Nebraska's
CARL MILTON ALDRICH
AND THE
ARBOR DAY SONG

Nebraska's
CARL MILTON ALDRICH
══ AND THE ══
ARBOR DAY SONG

RACHEL BRUPBACHER

FOREWORD BY TAMMY PARTSCH,
AUTHOR OF *IT HAPPENED IN NEBRASKA*

THE
History
PRESS

Published by The History Press
Charleston, SC
www.historypress.com

Copyright © 2022 by Rachel Brupbacher
All rights reserved

Front cover: The Arbor Lodge. *Author's collection.*

First published 2022

Manufactured in the United States

ISBN 9781467152990

Library of Congress Control Number: 2022937935

To Patricia Louise Aldrich Kelsay,
granddaughter of Carl Milton Aldrich but, to me, just plain "Aunt Pat"—
I love you dearly.

Abou Ben Adhem

Abou Ben Adhem (may his tribe increase!)
Awoke one night from a deep dream of peace,
And saw, within the moonlight in his room,
Making it rich, and like a lily in bloom,
An Angel writing in a book of gold:
Exceeding peace had made Ben Adhem bold,
And to the Presence in the room he said,
"What writest thou?" The Vision raised its head,
And with a look made of all sweet accord
Answered, "The names of those who love the Lord."
"And is mine one?" said Abou. "Nay, not so,"
Replied the Angel. Abou spoke more low,
But cheerly still; and said, "I pray thee, then,
Write me as one that loves his fellow-men."

The Angel wrote, and vanished. The next night
It came again with a great wakening light,
And showed the names whom love of God had blessed,
And, lo! Ben Adhem's name led all the rest!

James Henry Leigh Hunt
(1784–1859)

CONTENTS

FOREWORD

I t's a little embarrassing to admit this, but when Rachel first contacted
me with her book idea and a request to help track down some Nebraska
City information, I didn't know Carl Milton Aldrich. I've lived nearly
my whole life in Nebraska City and have even written a book about its history,
but that name was unfamiliar to me. In one of our first conversations, I
asked if Carl was related to the author Bess Streeter Aldrich (he is), but that
didn't shed any light on his identity.

However, the more I learned about Carl, from Rachel and through the
research she assigned me, the more intrigued I became. We are programmed
from an early age to learn the names of those whom society deems "important
people"—the ones whose names are on the sides of buildings, who often
appear in print, who have parks and schools named after them. Carl Milton
Aldrich was not one of those people, but his work in and for Nebraska City
built on their foundation.

Carl was only five when his parents moved away from Nebraska City.
He spent the next four decades trying to recapture the innocence and
simplicity of that small-town lifestyle even as he was becoming more and
more disillusioned with big business. Finally, in 1907, Carl and his family
returned to Nebraska City for good.

Rachel tells you the details of his life in the meantime, of his time in the
packing industry, his work with national policy and in community affairs.
She also paints a picture of the softer side of the working man, one who
wrote poetry, tended flowers and loved his mother.

In reading Rachel's book, I fell a little bit in love with Carl M. Aldrich. I admired his work ethic and integrity, and I respected his commitment to civic involvement. His love of nature and reverence of Arbor Day in particular are endearing and usually reserved for those of us who have lived in Nebraska City our whole lives, not just at the beginning and end.

Reading Carl's story reminds me there is more to a community than the bigwigs, the VIPs. What makes a community survive and thrive are those who work hard with honor, pursue their passions without glory and are true to themselves. Even if your name was forgotten, Carl, your footprint was not.

Tammy Partsch
Author of *It Happened in Nebraska* and *Nebraska City: Images of America*
March 2022

ACKNOWLEDGEMENTS

Where are all the photographs?"
This was a question that niggled incessantly at the back of my mind as I drafted the manuscript for *Nebraska's Carl Milton Aldrich and the Arbor Day Song*. For my previous book—another biography of another remarkable ancestor, California novelty architect Miles Minor Kellogg—I had had my choice of illustrations. The Kellogg family had left behind hundreds, if not thousands, of old portraits and sepia snapshots. For this project, however, I enjoyed no such good fortune.

I was grateful, of course, for what materials I did have—a solid, basic collection of memorabilia. I was more grateful still for the help that I received from relatives. And to these family members I would like to extend my heartfelt thanks: Mike Aldrich, Rob Aldrich, Karen Kelsay Davies (owner of the literary press Kelsay Books), Mary Donato, Susan Small Godfrey, Nancy Small Johnson, Patricia Aldrich Kelsay, the late Dr. Joan Patterson and Cheryl Hoiseth, Anne Strathie, Michael Swartz and Karen Aldrich Wikkerink. Few of these relatives had ever met me, yet all graciously shared whatever images or stories had survived in their respective branches of the Aldrich family tree.

However, even these invaluable contributions were, comparatively speaking, sparse. Where, I wondered, were all the many intimate photographs that affluent, turn-of-the-century families were so fond of snapping and sharing? And where, for that matter, was the voluminous correspondence that I knew Carl Milton Aldrich had engaged in? I was, frankly, baffled.

It was rather late in my research that I stumbled on an explanation. News coverage of the tragic 1934 burning of the Morton-Gregson livestock exchange building informed me that the conflagration had claimed many of his personal effects—items that had been "collected by him over a period of 40 years."[1]

As dismaying as this discovery was—the realization that a prolonged search for any further surviving artifacts from his life would most likely be a futile undertaking—it was helpful in confirming the necessity of seeking additional information from outside the Aldrich family circle. Fortunately, the conspicuous role that he played in meatpacking and political affairs ensured that such details could be found.

The organizations I would especially like to acknowledge for their contributions to my research are the Brucemore estate (for its images of T.M. Sinclair and the T.M. Sinclair & Co. packinghouse); the Linn County Historical Society (for information relating to the Aldriches' early years in Cedar Rapids); the Shelby County Historical and Genealogical Society (for its image of Tacketts' Tavern); the Citronelle Historical Preservation Society (for a copy of *All Roads Lead to Citronelle*); Nebraska City Tourism and Commerce (for its images of the wagon trains at the Missouri River, the Morton-Gregson parade float and St. Mary's Hospital); the Morton-James Public Library (for its image of St. Mary's Episcopal Church); the *Nebraska City News-Press* (for permission to reproduce poems and passages originally published in old issues of the Nebraska City newspapers); and History Nebraska (for its numerous images relating to the history of Nebraska City, Julius Sterling Morton and the Arbor Lodge).

I would also like to thank the following individuals for unstintingly donating their time and knowledge to the completion of this project: Jessica Peel-Austin, museum program manager at Brucemore; Kurk Shrader, executive director of the Bess Streeter Aldrich Foundation; Laureen Riedesel, former director of the Beatrice Public Library; Dr. George Gibson, retired professor of history and economics at Union College (NE); Donna Kruse, director of the Morton-James Public Library; and, most particularly, Tammy Partsch, Nebraska City historian and the author of *It Happened in Nebraska* (Globe Pequot, 2012), *Nebraska City: Images of America* (Arcadia Publishing, 2015) and *It Happened in Iowa* (TwoDot, 2017).

To all who have helped further my telling of Carl Milton Aldrich's life story, I thank you most sincerely. Please know that it has been immeasurably enriched by your generosity.

INTRODUCTION

Snow was swirling fiercely around the 1934 Plymouth. The heavy car doors opened cautiously as a young woman and her two children struggled out to brave the storm. It was not a good night to be outside, let alone on the road. It was cold—so cold that, on the drive down from Lincoln, the children had had to pile thick blankets over their laps in order to keep warm. The temperature inside the Plymouth had plummeted further whenever the boy had clambered out to scrape the windshield so that his mother could see to drive. Now, outside, the whipping flurries so blinded the travelers that they could barely make out the silhouette of the little town where they had stopped.

The woman had not expected difficulties. Floy Aldrich had made the drive from Lincoln to Hebron, Nebraska, many times, usually without mishap. It was a trip that meant much to both her and her children, Billy and Patsy, and also to her husband, Carl Milton Aldrich Jr. The Depression was on, and their life as a family had fragmented when Carl had accepted work with the Civilian Conservation Corps a year or so earlier. The weekends were now the Aldriches' only opportunity to spend some much-missed time together. Every now and then, Carl would journey to Lincoln to see his family, but more often than not, Floy and the children would make the drive down to the CCC Camp Hebron, where Carl was employed as supervisor.

This time, however, Floy had not consulted the weather about her travel plans. South of the capital, the Plymouth had driven straight into a blizzard. All that she and the children could do now was to shiver their way to the nearest hotel and seek accommodation for the night.

Even this seemingly straightforward plan was soon foiled. Times being what they were, the hotel's paramount concern was payment. The manager sternly issued his ultimatum: no money, no room. This created a genuine dilemma. Floy, who rarely carried large quantities of cash, did not have enough with her to meet the hotel's rates.

Fortunately, though, there was help available. Ringing up Camp Hebron, Floy explained the predicament to her husband. Carl Jr. then got in touch with his parents in Nebraska City. The next thing anyone knew, Mr. C.M. Aldrich Sr. was on the phone with the hotel manager, guaranteeing payment.

With some pride, Floy emphasized to her children the significance of what was occurring. So well known was their grandfather Aldrich that his word, given orally over the telephone—no signature required—was considered ample security by even the wariest of businessmen in the smallest and most obscure of Nebraska towns.

I had already spent several years researching for this book when my great-aunt Pat shared this childhood anecdote with me earlier this year. While I was delighted to have yet another vignette to round out my understanding of C.M. Aldrich's life and legacy, the story itself was merely confirmation of what I had come to realize some time ago—that he had been a "big wheel" in the state of Nebraska and, particularly, in his beloved hometown of Nebraska City.

Nevertheless, such a realization had been a long while in coming. Twelve years ago, I would have scarcely recognized C.M.'s name. And I had never so much as visited his native Nebraska. Four successive generations of Aldriches had once called the state home, and all had lived, at one point or another, in Nebraska City. However, by 2010, when I transferred to a small private college in Lincoln, many years had elapsed since a member of the family had lived in Nebraska's vast prairieland.

With all the self-preoccupation of a college senior, I initially took limited interest in our family's Nebraska heritage. My mother, on the other hand, was fascinated by it and took full advantage of my return to the old Aldrich stomping grounds. That November, she and my father drove hundreds of miles so that we could spend Thanksgiving together in Nebraska—and also do a little genealogical sleuthing on the side.

As we drove east from Lincoln, my mother briefed us on the few family history facts and figures that she had been able to collect. My grandpa, she explained, had been born in Lincoln, but his grandparents' home in Nebraska City—where we were now headed for the holidays—had also provided an important backdrop for his childhood. Grandpa's grandfather, she said somewhat hesitantly, had had something to do with Arbor Day there. At least she thought he had. The details escaped her.

Our first sight of Nebraska City was a bit underwhelming. "The Garden City" was a title that the town had well and truly earned years earlier, both because of its distinction as the birthplace of Arbor Day and because of the abundance and diversity of its plant life. Proud residents have conscientiously cultivated and maintained its reputation for natural beauty since 1872, when Julius Sterling Morton initiated the first observance of Arbor Day—the same holiday that C.M. himself so vigorously promoted.

But the Garden City does not show to best advantage in late fall. When my parents and I checked into the Lied Lodge that week, all of its deciduous trees were stripped bare of the lush foliage that gives the town its fabled Eden-like appearance during balmier months. Thus, in order to fully appreciate Nebraska City's charms and its significance to our family history, a bit of imagination was called for—imagination and also some local knowledge and historical context. I had neither knowledge nor context then, but by the time I returned several years later to conduct some in-person research, I had obtained both.

My journey of discovery began with an heirloom, a scrapbook that I found in my grandfather's house following his death in 2014. It was heavy with a collection of memorabilia that had been pasted or stapled onto its crisp, brown pages—calling cards and business cards; essays written in a child's struggling nineteenth-century cursive; formal business letters (a few of them personally signed by legendary "packers" Thomas McElderry Sinclair and Louis F. Swift); faded photographs; and tear-stained obituaries.

And then there were the poems. Lots of poems.

After thumbing through its pages several times, I concluded that this must be what was known as "Granny Aldrich's scrapbook." The scrapbook, though, was poorly named. It had, in fact, very little to do with Granny (my great-great-grandmother); its contents referred almost exclusively to her husband, C.M. Granny had compiled it, following his death, as a tribute to the life he had so richly lived.

For all that, the scrapbook supplied only a very rough sketch of his achievements. The information preserved within its covers hinted that C.M. had enjoyed a certain level of national prominence. Just exactly what his claims to distinction were, however, would require some in-depth exploration on my part. No one in the family, it seemed, remembered his story—most likely because he himself had modestly dismissed the significance of his own accomplishments.

C.M., I would come to realize, had been unpretentious. Consequently, his grandchildren—my grandfather and his younger sister Patsy, for example—had never felt in any way overawed by him. A down-to-earth, unassuming man, he had been, to them, simply "Granddaddy." His joint distinction as the manager of Nebraska City's major industry, the Morton-Gregson Packing Company, and as the author of the Arbor Day song that they sang every year in Nebraska's public schools had made but very slight impression on their minds. At the same time, stories from his extraordinary past had never reached their ears—stories about his early associations with United States vice president Charles Gates Dawes; his years as a national director of the Travelers' Protective Association; and his time as the manager of one of Swift & Company's most important packinghouses.

To his contemporaries, by contrast, the name C.M. Aldrich carried immense weight. His status, moreover, as one of Nebraska City's best-loved citizens was unquestioned. Besides helping to direct many of the town's most crucial business concerns, he poured thousands of his own dollars and spare hours into any new initiative that he thought might benefit his community. Just as significant, he labored energetically to ensure that Nebraska City retained its place in the nation's cultural consciousness by promoting its primary claim to fame—Arbor Day.

And yet his story—the story of one remarkable man and his equally remarkable town—sank into obscurity following his death in 1936.

Indeed, little today remains to remind current Nebraska City residents of C.M.'s long years of service. No parks or playgrounds or public buildings bear his name. Neither do any grand statues or other impressive monuments pay homage to his memory. C.M.'s grave and those of his family in Wyuka Cemetery are marked by modest, flat headstones, pressed inconspicuously into Nebraska's rich soil. His elegant house and garden, where he once lovingly tended his prize roses, have vanished. Only the rather tragic spectacle of the long-abandoned Morton-Gregson Co. buildings hint at the critical role that he played during the town's golden years.

Even C.M.'s contributions to Arbor Day have gone unacknowledged. The Arbor Day song, performed faithfully for decades at the annual celebrations held at J. Sterling Morton's Arbor Lodge mansion, has become such a fixed part of Arbor Day tradition that many have forgotten it ever had an author.

But that is, perhaps, just as C.M. himself would have wished it. His philosophy of life was of the homespun variety, and he took for his own ideal the common man—"plain earnest men" (in his own words) whose "crowning glory…were the simple virtues."[2] These men "did their work, the best they knew how," and "spoke not evil against their neighbors and left no one to nurse the sting of an unkind word."[3] Their "conception of duty was honest, consciencious [*sic*] performance of their daily task, loyalty to their town, and a religious love of home and children."[4] It was such men, to his way of thinking, who were the true heroes of the world. And Carl Milton Aldrich himself, I would venture to suggest, was one such hero.

Rachel Brupbacher
March 2022

PART I

The Story

CHAPTER 1

BIRTH OF A PIONEER

M y first distinct recollections," Carl Milton Aldrich would reflect in later years, "and about the only ones: Seeing the Indians file by a good many times; a good thrashing for throwing dead chickens in to the hog pen, and seeing the cows come up in the winter to lick the frost off the windowpane."[5]

Few though these memories were, the impression they left on his mind was enduring. Carl's pioneering days in the Nebraska Territory were of short duration, drawing to a close when he was only five years old. Yet his recollections of such early experiences would resonate within his consciousness and shape his imagination for the next forty years of his life. Even after he achieved acclaim in the cutthroat worlds of business and politics, his outlook would remain fundamentally influenced by his identity as a rugged pioneer. Moreover, it was his distinction as one of the first settlers' children to be born in Nebraska that he would prize above any other.

His parents, John and Mary Jane Aldrich, had come west several years prior to his birth.[6] Both native New Yorkers, they had married in 1855[7] before setting out the following year to help tame the wild prairies of the Nebraska Territory, recently established through the 1854 Kansas-Nebraska Act.

The decision to turn pioneer was not one that the Aldriches made lightly. John and Mary Jane were cultured young people who had spent at least part of their courtship organizing and running a literary society in Mary Jane's hometown of Sidney Plains, New York. The society had started up a

Nebraska City as it looked from the Iowa shore around 1859. *History Nebraska.*

periodical called *The Gleaner*; John had been its editor, and Mary Jane, their friends and her cousins had contributed pieces to each issue.[8] In cultivating such interests, the Aldriches were typical of Nebraska's early pioneers, whom Carl later characterized as "young people just married, all from good families, a good many of the women and girls from the best homes, and had had the advantage of a boarding school education, but started out with their husbands to build homes."[9]

To many genteel easterners, crossing half an expansive continent to forge new lives in a strange wilderness presented a daunting prospect. (After a year in the West, Mary Jane observed in a letter to her family that "after all Nebraska life has not been as rough as I expected.")[10] However, the Aldriches enjoyed a slight advantage over some of their fellow settlers. Trailblazing was already a well-established tradition in both John's and Mary Jane's families. The ancestries of each reached back to the infancy of the Thirteen Colonies and included some of the first Europeans to set foot in the New World and settle the fringes of its interior.

John's family enjoyed an especially long history in America. He was a descendant of *Mayflower* passenger William Brewster[11] and also of one George Aldrich, who had immigrated to the American colonies from his native England in the early 1600s.[12] George, a humble tailor, was the progenitor of the historic Aldrich family of America whose members would ultimately include United States president William Howard Taft; the writer Thomas Bailey Aldrich; long-serving United States senator Nelson W. Aldrich; Nelson's daughter Abby, who married the son of financier John D. Rockefeller; and small-town midwestern banker Charles Sweetzer Aldrich, whose wife, Bess Streeter Aldrich, became one of Nebraska's most beloved writers.[13]

Carl Milton Aldrich's great-grandparents Dr. Laurens Hull and Dorcas Ambler Hull. *Author's collection.*

But Mary Jane could also claim a fascinating lineage. On her mother's side, she was a granddaughter of the physician, manufacturer and politician Dr. Laurens Hull.[14] Widely regarded as a self-made man,[15] Dr. Hull had served as president of the New York State Medical Society and as a member of the New York State Senate.[16] His own father, Dr. Titus Hull, had served as a surgeon during the Revolutionary War,[17] during which same conflict Laurens's father-in-law, David Ambler, had been a minuteman and a member of the Connecticut Committee of Safety.[18]

Mary Jane's paternal grandfather was an even more extraordinary individual. Witter Johnston had been a teenager when, in 1772, he and his father, the Edinburgh-educated Reverend William Johnston, ventured into the New York interior and established one of the first settlements in the Susquehanna River Valley—the place that would become Sidney Plains.[19] Together, father and son constructed a log cabin there, and then the reverend left Witter to fend for himself, with only the local Indian tribes to assist him in case of emergency,[20] until he returned a year later with the rest of the family.[21]

The Johnstons remained on their new homestead for only a short while. Hostilities soon broke out between Great Britain and the American colonies, culminating in the Revolutionary War. A subsequent altercation between the Reverend Johnston and the Mohawk chief and British sympathizer Joseph Brant left the family feeling threatened and convinced them that they would be safer living near Cherry Valley, New York. The fort there, the Johnstons believed, would offer adequate protection against a potential onslaught from the British.[22] The move to Cherry Valley, however, was a mistake—and one for which they nearly paid with their lives. The Johnstons narrowly escaped slaughter in the infamous 1778 Cherry Valley massacre, led by Brant himself and the notorious Captain Walter Butler.[23] While his parents and siblings fled to the safety of the woods and hid there overnight, Witter, by that time a young man, helped to successfully defend the fort.[24] Witter proved himself to be an able soldier, and in the years that followed, he rose to the rank of colonel in the Continental army, dining with George Washington on one occasion. At war's end, he and the rest of the family returned to Sidney Plains, where they rebuilt their property and remained for years to come.[25]

Recollecting stirring stories like these heartened John and Mary Jane as they followed in their pioneering forebears' footsteps. Nevertheless, they might not have given up the comparative civilization of rural New York for the rigors of the Wild West had they not had the reassurance of family companionship in Nebraska. Also heading there around this time was Mary Jane's younger bachelor brother Laurens.[26]

An unflagging idealism fueled the young couple's enthusiasm. Their interest in pioneering was not based solely on a self-centered desire to "get powerful rich"—a destiny that Mary Jane laughingly prophesied for her brother Laurens.[27] Their purposes were somewhat more altruistic; religious fervor unquestionably contributed to their plans.

Surviving correspondence and other records make plain that the Aldriches were equally matched as practicing Christians. Mary Jane's biographer and sister, Dorcas "Dora" Johnston Turner, emphasized the early interest that Mary Jane took in all church-related affairs. Dora noted how, at age seventeen, her sister "united with the church in Sidney, not going with others of her own age, but alone, while her companions stood aloof. One proof that she was in the church for work was the organization of a missionary society among the children of the Sunday School."[28]

John took his faith just as seriously. Far from being a hen-pecked husband bending to a zealous wife's will, he was a dedicated Sabbath keeper by personal choice and conviction. Writing to her family in 1857, Mary Jane remarked on the practice of Sabbath observance in Nebraska (or lack thereof): "You must know that in Nebraska no man cuts wood for a day ahead. It is not fashionable—it is cut when you want it. There are a few, my own husband among the number, who try to cut on Saturday their Sunday's wood, but it is not the majority of the people, I can assure you."[29]

Apparently under the auspices of a home missionary society,[30] John and Mary Jane intended to work as educators in Otoe County's newly incorporated Nebraska City.[31] "Beautifully situated on the bank of the Missouri River," the town was positioned "about sixty miles south of Omaha…and 110 miles north of St. Joseph, Mo."[32]

The romantic prospect of becoming an ennobling influence in a rustic western town held understandable appeal. However, the Aldriches may not have reckoned with the competing ambitions of other well-educated easterners. John and Mary Jane faced, in short, stiff competition. Other Nebraska City residents entertained teaching aspirations and were establishing schools in the area around this time.[33]

Such a glut of would-be educators presumably compelled John and Mary Jane to reconsider their plans. Mary Jane was eventually able to fulfill her teaching dreams by holding both a regular school[34] and a Sabbath school[35] in their own home. John, meanwhile, as the one responsible for their financial support, had to pursue other employment.

Back in New York, John had worked as a salesman.[36] He had, however, also acquired manual skills. In 1856, during their first winter in Nebraska, John obtained work in a sawmill owned by a man named Squires.[37] The mill was located south of Nebraska City and, as Mary Jane described it, "across the river."[38] By the time John returned to work for Squires the

An artist's rendering of Nebraska City, circa 1860. *History Nebraska.*

following winter, the mill had been relocated to a place intriguingly called Bloody Island.[39]*

John's promotion to head sawyer in late 1857 came as joyful news, especially to his wife.[40] Writing to her mother, Mary Jane conveyed her feelings of happy anticipation in run-on sentences:

> *He is to be head sawyer this winter—has $10 per week until the 1st of January + $1.75 per day from that time until the 1st of April or about $45 a month + a house to live in + our wood will cost a mere nothing except the trouble of getting, which will be much less than where we are now as we shall live right in the woods + it will be very much sheltered from wind + storms. Meat is getting much cheaper, + I think that $3.00 a week will furnish our table plentifully so that, if our health is spared, I think we shall do pretty well.*[41]

It was the promise of a house near the mill that meant the most to Mary Jane. She and John had been living in Otoe City,† a community of hamlet proportions situated about five miles south of Nebraska City. Their neighbors had been kind, but sickness—and death—had been rampant in recent months.[42] Mary Jane had frequently succumbed to illness, and with her husband away working on the island, she had at times fallen into despondency.[43] Having a house near John's place of work meant that they could be together, no matter what befell them.

Their move to Bloody Island that fall, however, was not without complications.

Neither John nor Mary Jane had been overwhelmed by the prospect of living at a distance from an organized settlement like Nebraska City or even tiny Otoe City. Both, after all, had been reared in small rural communities. New to their experience, though, were the extremes of Nebraska weather. How treacherously it could deal with unsuspecting newcomers they, like so many others, had already learned, to their great dismay.

The Aldriches had arrived in Nebraska just in time to live through the very worst it could offer. Their first winter—that of 1856—had shaken the self-confidence of many early settlers. The Andreas *History of Nebraska*, an authoritative 1882 text on state history, paints a distressingly vivid picture:

---

* Bloody Island is believed to have been located in the middle of the Missouri River and to have disappeared, at least as a separate landmass, following an eastward rerouting of the river by the U.S. Army Corps of Engineers.
† Otoe City was also known for many years as Minersville.

Those who came to [this] section of Nebraska…as early as 1854, or 1855, will remember the balmy, springlike, "first winters" which deceived many into believing that they had found a land where summer reigned perpetual. They will also remember how dearly the injudicious paid for their mistake, in supposing that what had been necessarily would be, during the terrible cold winter which began on December 1, 1856, "freezing into ninety solid blocks of ice all the days of that month and the succeeding ones of January and February, 1857." Many lives were lost in the storms of that period. Deep snows covered the whole earth, and game, which before the year 1857 had been abundant—venison saddles being sold at $1.50, and dressed wild turkeys at 75 cents each—perished from cold and hunger. Deer ran through the streets of Nebraska City seeking safety from wolves, which followed them on the ice crusted snow, which the sharp feet of the fleeing kine cut through.[44]

Living through such an experience could not but make a lasting impression on John and Mary Jane's consciousness. Thus, it was with extreme caution that they made preparations to move their household across the ice-encrusted Missouri River that winter of 1857. Mary Jane described their ordeal in a letter to her father dated December 17:

It is now some 10 or 11 weeks since we first thought of coming to the Island for the winter. I do not remember exactly what time in October I was taken sick, but the day that I came home sick with bilious fever from Mrs. Lee's was the day that John came down to Mr. Squire's + engaged to work in the mill. He was to go to work the next Monday (this was Wednesday) + in two weeks, they were to have a house for us to move into. On account of my illness, he did not come down on Monday but remained in Otoe until Thursday Eve. He worked in the mill Friday + Saturday morn., came home sick with quinsy, was home all the next week, + the week following came home on Friday. Mr. Squires had run the carriage back onto the saw + broken it, + the lumber for our house was still unsawed. But they were in hopes to get a new saw the next day. The new saw, however, did not make its appearance until a week from the following Monday. The first week after the new saw made its appearance, John put up a house for us to live in, or it was put up by somebody, + Saturday night John came home with a light heart in hopes that we could move the 1st of the next week. Sabbath night it was very cold, + we hoped that the Missouri would be bridged with ice for our freight but not so. It was cold + the anchor ice kept *running so that crossing was a very difficult matter, but the channel of the river was not to be frozen over that time. Tuesday night the ice blocked both above + below Otoe, leaving the channel clear with a wide strip of ice along either shore. Wednesday there were several skiff loads of shingles brought on a hand sled across the ice loaded in a skiff + landed on the ice on the other side, + we concluded to pack up just what we could not do without + move in a skiff Thursday morning. Wednesday night the south wind blew strong, but some gentlemen who crossed in the morning of Thursday assured John that the ice was strong, + he + Mr. Dewey began to carry a load down to the skiff. A team was not to be had. The stove went first with some other things, but to make the stove light, they took off the doors + griddles. They took the stove across + landed it on the shore thinking that the heaviest was now across the ice. The second load I came over, but instead of unloading anything from the skiff, John, seeing that, while they had been absent—a portion of some 15 minutes—the ice had settled two or three inches, concluded to conduct me across to the shore. We did not walk slow, I can assure you—splash, splash went the water—+ we stepped spryer + spryer. When we had crossed that part of the ice which had settled under the water, Mr. Dewey called to John not to recross for the ice was too tender to allow of drawing the goods across on the sled. He would take the things back + take care of them. We went on + reached the shore, + there we were fairly <u>astraddle</u> of the Missouri River, our stove, with not a griddle or a piece of pipe with it, that + one or two pails on the Iowa side with us, everything else in the boat going back to Otoe or in our little house that we had just left. We went up to the cabin of a Mr. Doyle not far from the river, + there I dried my skirts that had got wet crossing on the ice. Fortunately, I had on my over socks over my rubbers so that my feet + ankles were scarcely dampened. Mrs. Doyle gave us some dinner, + then arose the question what shall we do? There was no team to be had, + Mrs. D. had a house full + more, too, of men boarders. I did not want to stay there, + John was unwilling that I should try + walk to the Island—a distance of two miles + a half. I had had two chills, with an interval of two weeks between each one, since my first one that I wrote to you of, + the next day was the time for another, if it should choose to come, + John feared that if I walked to the Island that, together with getting my clothes damp on the ice, would be sure to bring on Ague. But I was certain it would not, + as my clothes were now well dried, thanks to a capacious fireplace, it was finally concluded that we take up our line of march. This was Thursday the 26th of November. Thanksgiving Day!!! I did wish you could see us as we trudged on in the*

Wagon trains at the Missouri River in 1859. *Nebraska City Tourism and Commerce.*

mud—such mud as is found only in the West. I had a small farm hanging to each foot. Still, on we went. When we came to the slough which divides the Island from the mainland, we found that considerably higher than when John crossed it on a rail the Saturday before. The rail was washed away, + now the best we could do was to find a shallow spot + wade it. This was soon found, + John walked through the water, carrying me in his arms. I was glad, then, that he was the stronger of the two, or I should probably have been obliged to carry him. We reached Mr. Squire's about 3 o'clock, just as I began to feel tired—thankful enough to get there even though we could not go to housekeeping. We were <u>with</u> <u>each</u> <u>other</u>.[45]

The young couple's newly risen spirits soon flagged, however. Squires's wife did not welcome her unexpected guests with open arms. To the contrary, her "delicacy," as Mary Jane noted, discouraged boarders.[46] Nor was that all. The next morning John's employer abruptly announced that he "no longer needed his services. He told him he had no use for the house which had been put up for him, + he could go into it, + when he had work for him, he would let him have it."[47] John responded by informing Squires firmly that "that was not the way he <u>hired</u> <u>out</u>."[48] He did not waste time arguing the issue but instead immediately began seeking alternative employment.[49]

The Aldriches' adventure was not yet concluded, though. It was some days before they were reunited with their belongings. Mary Jane explained:

> *Sabbath we heard that the river was clear of ice + were in hopes we could move Monday. Monday morning John went over to the west side of the Island where there is another sawmill + engaged to work for 1.25 per day with a house to live in, thinking it better to do that than be idle for some time in search of higher wages. It was doubtful, too, about getting great wages now for it is late to engage for the winter, + we are feeling the hard times here a little. I suppose that it was because John received the highest wages of any of the hands that Mr. Squires discharged him as he began to feel the pressure of the times.* To our disappointment, the river was on Monday again full of ice + continued so all the week. Wednesday I was taken with ague having taken some cold on Monday, which, slight though it was, set me to shaking. John went to work at Ley's Mill the days he did not spend in going to Otoe to try + get our goods over, but he came over to Mr. Squires' every night for the boarding house here was already overflowing. I had a chill every day after Wednesday, + Sabbath morning John said he was going to Otoe once more, + if the river was clear as it was the Sabbath before, he <u>should</u> <u>come</u> <u>to</u> <u>the</u> <u>conclusion</u> that the Lord favored his moving on that day. He went, found the river clear, + moved over two skiff loads. Monday morning it rained, but as I expected a chill about eleven + when the fever is on, I have such a severe headache that I like to keep quiet + would be afraid of taking cold after the sweat, we concluded to come down in the morning. John got a team, + it stopped raining a little while, + we moved into our own house once more—two as thankful children as you ever saw.[50]*

Mary Jane's relief at finding herself safely installed in their new home found expression through humor:

> *We are now at last as we hope,* [she informed her father] *settled for the winter in our home on the Island. It is a little house, 12 by 10½ feet with a real Gothic roof, + that gives us quite a chamber, + under the house is a cellar, perhaps 6 feet square. I tell Mr. Aldrich we no longer live in a shanty, but we reside in a "Gothic cottage." True, it is small, but it is*

---

* The Panic of 1857 marked a nationwide economic downturn.

*built in Gothic style, that is certain, + who ever heard of a Gothic shanty?
Therefore, it <u>must</u> be a cottage.*[51]

Precisely how long the Aldriches remained on Bloody Island is not easy
to ascertain. Raymond E. Dale's meticulously researched *Otoe County Pioneers*
reports that, over a period of years, John worked in sawmills in Otoe County
and Nemaha County.[52] J. Sterling Morton's *Illustrated History of Nebraska* adds
detail, indicating that John "owned and operated a saw mill" on Bloody
Island.[53] Carl Aldrich himself indicated that, by 1860, his parents were
living on a farm five miles south of Nebraska City.[54*] In any case, what is
almost certain is that the Aldriches continued to live on the land (rather than
in town) and to farm on a small scale during the remainder of their near-
decade residence in Nebraska.

It was, in fact, around 1857 that Nebraska settlers began to turn their
minds seriously to agriculture. The Andreas *History* reports:

> *Up to this time the thought of persistent attempts to cultivate the soil had
> not been favorably or generally entertained. "Cain had been a farmer and
> came out badly, and agriculture was regarded as rather a plebian vocation
> at best." Moreover there were legends to the effect that Nebraska could never
> become a commonwealth of farmers. But at this time, in the words of
> Hon. J. Sterling Morton, "it was discovered that a man with some mind
> and muscle could deposit eight quarts of Indian corn in a well plowed
> acre of Otoe County land, and by reasonably careful cultivation, and the
> co-operation of sunbeams and raindrops, gather in the autumn anywhere
> from fifty to eighty bushels of the cereal, from the same acre—and have all
> the land left."*[55]

Cultivating crops under Nebraska's unpredictable weather conditions
was, nevertheless, challenging. A drought two years later, in the summer of
1859, left many of the Aldriches' fellow settlers devastated. According to the
Andreas *History*:

> *Little or no rain fell during the entire season, and crops of all kinds through-
> out the entire West were unusually light. As a consequence, the cost of
> living, though unreasonably high before, was still further advanced, and
> the many in reduced circumstances who depended upon the produce of their*

---

* In a 1929 interview with the *Nebraska Daily News-Press*, Carl identified the place of his birth
in 1860 as a locality known as "the Meadville First Farm."

land for their support, suffered considerable deprivation. The succeeding season however, by some unknown law of compensation, was all or more than could be asked.[56]

It was at the end of one parched summer that the Aldriches endured their own tragedy. In September 1858, Mary Jane gave birth to their first child, a son, only for him to die, unnamed, after three days.[57] Further heartache came two years later when just one of the twins that Mary Jane delivered on August 26 survived the day.[58] The boy, whom they named Carl Milton, lived; his sister did not. The next year, the Aldriches welcomed another child, their daughter Lucette, this time with unblemished joy.[59]

Carl's birth year of 1860, as it happened, marked another event—one whose consequences would reverberate throughout the country for the next half decade. That fall, the election of Abraham Lincoln to the office of United States president whirled up a storm that would culminate, the following spring, in the outbreak of the War Between the States.

In geographic terms, Nebraska was far removed from most of the Civil War's bloody battlegrounds. Nevertheless, Lincoln's election, the subsequent outbreak of war and—above all—the "slavery question" presented unique dilemmas for early Nebraska society.

Few places were as divided in opinion over slavery as the newly established Nebraska Territory, where the legality of slaveholding was still hotly debated.* In the years leading up to the war, only twelve slaves were known to be resident in Nebraska City.[60] But the presence—or, rather, disappearance—of even such a comparatively small number was enough to drive a wedge between local abolitionists and their slaveholding or secessionist-sympathizing neighbors. Much to the annoyance of their masters, nearly half of the slaves escaped to freedom with the help of Otoe County's efficient Underground Railroad.[61] Ultimately, Nebraska's antislavery population appears to have exceeded its proslavery faction. In May 1860, companies of troops began to organize throughout the future state to protect it "against the incursions of the 'secessionists.'"[62]

And yet there was more behind this military mobilization than contention over the slavery question—or even the war itself. Nebraskans were just as anxious to arm themselves against a possible backlash from discontented Native American tribes. The United States government had earlier begun relocating (or removing entirely from Nebraska) groups of Cheyenne,

---

* The Kansas-Nebraska Act had effectively repealed the Missouri Compromise, which had prohibited slavery north of the 36° 30' latitude in the western territories.

Omaha, Pawnee and Sioux. Some of these tribes, it was feared, might be tempted to exploit the apparent fracturing of the United States and wreak revenge on the settlers who had displaced them from their homelands.[63]

Such concerns were not unreasonable; Indian warfare was far from a thing of the past. The Sioux Wars, in fact, had scarcely begun. In 1854, the Grattan Massacre had resulted in the slaughter and mutilation of a detachment of United States soldiers in present-day Wyoming. A year later, the United States Army had taken punitive action against the Brulé Lakotas along the Platte River in Nebraska. Further violence, an attack of Sioux against settlers in neighboring Iowa, had occurred in 1857, the year after John and Mary Jane came west.

Threats of Indian raids, however, were often magnified in newspapers back East. Mary Jane found herself compelled to reassure relatives in New York of their comparative safety. "When you read of Indian troubles in our territory," she wrote them, "don't be afraid of our being 'skulped' as a man said in here the other day. I do not think we are in danger."[64]

Indeed, Otoe County settlers need not have worried. The Andreas *History* recorded only a single "incident." In the summer of 1861, there was "an Indian scare of considerable size"[65] that "resulted in sending the troops on a flying trip through the western part of the county."[66] This "scare" proved to be a false alarm. On arrival, the men found "that the women and children of the tribe had been placed near the settlement for protection from the Sioux, and the warriors had gone on their regular buffalo hunt."[67]

Like their countrymen, John and Mary Jane took sides in the contentious issues of the day. Both supported Lincoln and the Republican Party. (This party had recently been organized as a result of opposition to the Kansas-Nebraska Act, which left open the issue of slavery to popular sovereignty.) John participated in the local February 1860 caucus and in the county convention held later that year in September.[68] As Northerners as well as Republicans, the Aldriches aligned themselves with the cause of the Union. Like many men in the Nebraska Territory, John did not actually "go to war" but instead did his part by serving as a private with the district Camp Creek Guards.[69]

Relatives' military allegiances fortified the Aldriches' loyalties to the Union. In 1862, Mary Jane's brother Witter enlisted in the 144th New York Infantry.[70] He was later severely wounded at the 1865 Battle of James Island in South Carolina.[71] The war was also the making of an outstanding military career for Mary Jane's first cousin Henry Baxter (1821–1873). Henry, like Mary Jane, was born in Sidney Plains,[72] but he had moved with his parents to Michigan at a young age.[73] A former '49er,[74] Henry served in the Civil War with distinction. He fought valiantly in many of the war's bloodiest and most decisive battles, including those at Fredericksburg, Chancellorsville and Gettysburg, and eventually earned the rank of brigadier general.[75]

But as a general rule, the war seemed far removed from the quiet Nebraska prairies. Daily life out West had, after all, its own troubles—particularly those of the financial variety. A few pioneers began to amass fortunes early on, but most, like the Aldriches, did not. They were, as Carl would one day describe them, as "poor as Job's Turkeys."[76] John and Mary Jane's possessions were minimal—in 1860, their total personal property was valued at $100[77]—and the standard Nebraska log cabin consisted of one or two tiny, stuffy rooms. The interior of the Aldrich home was similar to that of a neighboring family who had merely "a packing box for a table, two chairs and some small boxes for other chairs."[78] "We don't have much," Mary Jane wrote to family.[79] But they could get by. "We don't suffer for want of anything," she insisted reassuringly.[80]

Loneliness was another trial familiar to the early pioneers. Families generally lived at distances of five or ten miles from each other.[81] However, John and Mary Jane interpreted this apparent drawback as a blessing in disguise. They appreciated how prohibitive distances like these actually helped to foster warm friendships among the settlers, encouraging them to cherish all the more the relatively rare occasions when they could get together and enjoy some good fellowship.

With neighbors depending on one another for basic survival, such warm friendships proved invaluable. One night, when Carl was ill, a neighbor came to help Mary Jane care for the little boy. "Doctor Bowen blistered my throat for the croup," Carl recollected much later, "and [the neighbor woman] carried me in her arms a good part of the night until I got to breathing and could go to sleep."[82]

All told, it was a good life. And it was a life that John and Mary Jane's son would endeavor, for the rest of his days, to recapture.

CHAPTER 2

BACK TO THE WEST

To the West, to the West,
   To the land of the free,
Where the mighty Missouri
   Rolls down to the sea
Where a man is a man,
   If he's willing to toil
And the humblest may gather
   The fruit of his toil.

Come along, Come along,
   Make no delay,
Come from every nation
   Come from every way.
Our land it is broad enough
   So have no alarm
For Uncle Sam is rich enough
   To give us all a farm.[83]

So sang Mary Jane Aldrich[84] as she reared her children, tended her garden, tidied the family cabin and prepared food for the table. It was a popular song—beguiling in the simplicity of its tune and the uplifting sentiments of its lyrics. The words, however, were deceptive. "Uncle Sam" might have been "rich enough" to distribute farms, right and

A view of Nebraska City looking northwest from Kearney Hill. This photo was taken circa 1870, a few years after the Aldriches' departure from the area. *History Nebraska.*

left, through the 1862 Homestead Act, but even such a bounteous "gift" of 160 acres came with a price—that of living on the land as well as cultivating and improving it for a minimum of five years. Nor was it adequate to ensure financial solvency for the settlers who soon flooded the American West, let alone for those men and women who had already been toiling in the Nebraska Territory since the passage of the Kansas-Nebraska Act eight years earlier.

The Aldriches were among those who failed to thrive.

Despite their best efforts, John and Mary Jane's various ventures on the Nebraska frontier did not bear lasting fruit. They had been laboring there for nearly a decade when, in 1865—the same year the Civil War concluded—they packed up their small family and embarked on a weeks-long journey back to Mary Jane's hometown of Sidney Plains, New York.[85] There they remained for a year as they drew up their plans for the future.[86] Responsible for the well-being of two children, they exercised caution in determining their next step.

A future in Sidney Plains was apparently impractical. Lack of available land was undoubtedly one factor that had prompted John and Mary Jane to leave New York in the first place. The Reverend William Johnston, Mary Jane's great-grandfather, had been judicious in drawing up his will. He had left his

Carl Aldrich, age four, with his sister Luta, age three, about a year before they left Nebraska. *Author's collection.*

substantial acreage divided equally among his numerous children, male and female alike.[87] Subdivisions like this could not continue indefinitely, however, as the Johnston clan steadily expanded over subsequent generations.[88] Mary Jane's aunt Lois, the mother of General Henry Baxter, was one relative who had likely found herself gently elbowed out. She and her husband, Levi Baxter, had left New York in the 1830s, ultimately establishing themselves in Michigan.[89] John and Mary Jane now found themselves in a similar quandary. Like her aunt Lois, Mary Jane was one of many children. Besides sisters, she had three brothers, the youngest of whom would remain in Sidney Plains to work the land for his own support.[90]

In the end, John and Mary Jane set their sights on the West once more. Relatives were thriving in Cedar Rapids, Iowa, and they convinced the Aldriches to try their fortunes there. In 1866, they left New York once more and headed back to the West—this time, with Iowa as their destination.[91]

Situated farther east than Nebraska and incorporated several years earlier, Cedar Rapids had had more time to develop than Nebraska City had. The older city would, John and Mary Jane hoped, offer more favorable employment opportunities. In this hope, however, they were disappointed. According to Mary Jane's sister Dora, the move to Cedar Rapids did little to improve their financial circumstances: "There were months when plans failed, and life was down to the level of necessities, other months when work to supply the daily needs filled all the week-days, and Sunday was a day of rest."[92] The Aldriches raised their own pears and beans to save on expenses, and both John and Mary Jane worked in order to keep their small family afloat.[93] While John found unsteady employment at the Cedar Rapids Paper Mill,[94] Mary Jane added to her childrearing and housekeeping responsibilities by running a school in their own home.[95] Carl and his sister Lucette (familiarly known as Luta) received instruction there alongside five other children whose parents, like Mary Jane, deprecated the education that was available in Cedar Rapids' public schools.[96]

These formal school hours did not, however, account for the sum total of Carl and Luta's education. Mary Jane did not believe that mastery of the three Rs rendered a child's education complete. She took pains to give her son and daughter rigorous moral and spiritual instruction as well. This she did by reading aloud from a scrapbook that she had begun compiling around the time of their departure from Nebraska. Into the pages of a fat "industrial book" she pasted stories, songs, poems and other items that she considered edifying to the minds of impressionable young children.[97] Most of these, in keeping with the cultural climate of the day, had very strong didactic or religious overtones.*

It was possibly during his homeschooled years that Carl composed his earliest extant essay. Reproduced here (complete with aberrant mechanics), it suggests an attentive and pragmatic interest in the world around him—a trait that would serve Carl well in almost any endeavor he would undertake as an adult:

---

* Carl came to love this homemade storybook. On his mother's death many years later, the first thing he did was to locate it and inscribe within its covers, "This book was compiled by my mother when we were young children—a loving work for our own good."

House

A house is a very nice thing to live in., The different parts of a hous are made of different materials, such as stone mortar wood line + brick, of course different kinds work men are employed in building a house. The first thing toward building a house is to dig a cellar or trench to lay the stone in for a foundation the different men emploued in building a house are the stone + brick mason if the house is brick are employed more than any other kind of workmen, in frame houses carpenters are employ more than any other's, the different parts of a house are the cellar, kitchen dining + setting room parlor bedroons pantry closet + attic the different colors used in painting a house are white yellow brown red + lead color the window shutters are generally green[98]

After a few years at home, Carl continued his education at the local public schools.[99] It was presumably during this time that he composed the only other piece of childhood writing that has survived the passage of time. Another scholastic essay, it provides fascinating insight into the average American schoolchild's knowledge of the solar system during the mid-1800s:

Sun

The sun is supposed to be the center of the solar system and is an immense globe or sphere surrounded by an intensely hot atmosphere composed of burning gasses. It is nearly 95 000 000. of miles from the earth. With regard to our earth the sun is stationary, but it's supposed by some to have two motions; one on its axis and one around some center and which is the same to it, as it is to the earth. With regard to the distance of the sun from the earth it is estimated that a railroad train moveing at the rate of 20 miles an hour would be 500 years in going from the earth to the sun. With regard to size the sun is 1 400 000. times as large as the earth, which is one of the eight larger plannets which revolv around the sun. Plannets are heavenly bodies which revolv around the sun 104 of these plannets have been discovered some of which perform annual revolutions around the sun while others visit him from the unbounded region of space Eight of these plannets are larger than the others The eight larger ones are Mercury. Venus. Earth Mars Jupiter Saturn Uranus and Neptune, The sun is 738 times as large as all of these plannets and their moons taken together. There great black spots on the sun although we cannot se them with the naked eye they are however some times so large that we can see them through a piece of smoked glass, different persons suppose different things about these spots but the theory which is generaly accepted is that the sun is an immense globe or sphere surrounded by an intensly hot atmosphere composed of burning gasses and that these blazes breaking into jets we sometimes get a glance at the interior, It is said that a man that would weight 200 lbs on the earth would if carried to the sun weigh 3,380 lbs or nearly 2½ Tons[100]

Carl's extracurricular activities included attending church with his family on Sundays and, as he grew older, participating in sporting events. (In due course, he would become a member of the Cedar Rapids Boat Club.)[101] His childhood ended, however, a few months short of his sixteenth birthday. On May 1, 1876, he left his school days behind forever and started work as an office boy at T.M. Sinclair & Co., a local meatpacking company whose operations had begun several years earlier.[102]

In nineteenth-century America, it was not unheard of for a middle-class boy to leave school in his mid-teens. This was common practice even in affluent families. A university education was not seen as essential by the wealthy—desirable, perhaps, if a son demonstrated academic ability but by no means necessary in order to hold or attain a certain social or financial status. For those less affluent or well connected, however, entering the workforce at a young age was typically a matter of financial necessity. A case in point was Carl's second cousin, future retail magnate Harry Selfridge

(circa 1856–1947). Around the time that Carl entered T.M. Sinclair & Co.'s employment, Harry was getting his own start in the retail business at the Chicago department store that would become known as Marshall Field & Company.[103] Harry, a nephew of General Henry Baxter and the only surviving child of Mary Jane's cousin Lois Baxter Selfridge, had been raised entirely by his mother, his father having abandoned the family during his service in the Union army.[104] By working as a schoolteacher in her family's adopted hometown of Jackson, Michigan, Lois had supported herself and her son until Harry was a teenager and able to go to work.[105]

Carl at age seventeen, a year after he began working for T.M. Sinclair & Co. *Author's collection.*

As in the case of Harry, it was almost certainly financial necessity that propelled Carl into the workforce at fifteen. Circumstantial evidence

The T.M. Sinclair & Co. packinghouse in 1878. By this time, Carl had been with the company for two years. *Farmstead Foods Collection of Brucemore, Inc.*

suggests that John Aldrich's health was deteriorating. By this time, he was no longer employed at the paper mill[106] but was working at a less physically taxing job as a clerk in a leather goods store.[107] Carl would have been distinctly aware of the uncertain state of his family's finances, which grew only more precarious following the birth of his younger brother John Jr. in 1872.[108] In later years, Mary Jane would proudly recall how, on every payday, Carl would dutifully hand over his entire wages of three dollars[109] to his father, without ever asking to keep any of it for himself as spending money.[110] The family would come to rely increasingly on Carl's wages after his father suffered a complete collapse in health in 1879, resulting in a nearly fatal illness.[111]

Yet however grave the circumstances were that thrust Carl into the grown-up, workaday world, his future was far from bleak. He could not have been more fortunate in what was to become his life's career. The meatpacking industry was booming in post–Civil War America, and those who succeeded in the business were destined for fame and wealth.

He was likewise lucky in his first employer, T.M. Sinclair & Co.

Prior to the Civil War, the meatpacking industry was concentrated in Cincinnati (known as "Porkopolis").[112] This changed, however, in the war's aftermath. As sprawling railroad networks made overland transport preferable to that via water and as packinghouse owners sought to achieve more efficient processing of their livestock by establishing slaughterhouses closer to the ranches of the West, the center of American packing activity shifted westward.[113] The then-comparatively modest and muddy town of Chicago, located at a major railroad intersection, soon dominated the scene.[114]

Among the new plants to emerge during this westward trend was T.M. Sinclair & Co. Its founder, though, was no newcomer to the business. Thomas McElderry Sinclair (1842–1881) belonged to an Irish American meatpacking dynasty that had opened its first packinghouse in Ireland in 1832.[115] After a fire destroyed the family's New York City plant, Sinclair had wisely taken the advice of a former employee to make the most of the industry's movement west and, in 1871, had opened his plant in Cedar Rapids.[116]

Thomas McElderry Sinclair, founder of T.M. Sinclair & Co. *From* Semi-Centennial 1871–1921: T.M. Sinclair & Co. Ltd.

Due in part to its refrigeration facilities (it was the second in the country to make use of ice refrigeration)[117] and in part to an abundance of resident immigrant labor, T.M. Sinclair & Co. soon had the largest packinghouse in Iowa.[118] Within less than a decade of its opening, the plant was the fourth largest in the world.[119] Significantly, it was in T.M. Sinclair & Co.'s own specialty—pork packing—that Carl would go on to earn for himself a name as one of America's foremost experts.

T.M. Sinclair's reputation as a leading "packer" was matched by his reputation for philanthropy. The Sinclairs were devoutly religious and well known for their dedication to promoting "good works." Sinclair established a Sunday school for his workers and also served as a missionary to the Native American Ponca tribe.[120] His wife, meanwhile, organized what became the Third Presbyterian Church.[121]

It was the Sinclair family's piety and charitable activities that most likely sealed the approval of Carl's mother when he first sought employment with T.M. Sinclair & Co. Indeed, it may have been Mary Jane Aldrich's own prominence as a dynamic social reformer that initially brought her son to the Sinclairs' attention. A couple of years before Carl left school, she had begun to attract national attention through her work as a temperance activist.

Due largely to the abysmal failure of the federally mandated 1920s Prohibition legislation, the temperance movement has long been regarded as an embarrassing epoch in United States history. The women who took on the "Demon Liquor" are often painted as meddling busybodies who were intent on depriving their husbands, sons and brothers of a well-deserved and sociable glass of beer at the end of a hard day's work. Such depictions, however, are misleading.

The issue of temperance—or moderation in (if not total abstinence from) imbibing alcohol—had been smoldering in America from the earliest years of the country's settlement. By the early 1800s, drinking alcoholic beverages (especially hard liquors like whiskey) had become commonplace to the point that it was regarded almost as a necessity of life.[122] There were practical reasons, of course, for such widespread consumption. Water was often contaminated, milk spoiled easily and, for a long time, coffee and tea were beyond the budget of the average American. Alcohol seemed like the most logical choice of beverage.[123]

Nevertheless, the almost perpetual state of intoxication in which many Americans found themselves resulted in irresponsible, if not outright dangerous, behavior. This had devastating consequences both for the overall moral fabric of society and, more particularly, for the families of the alcoholics themselves. Throughout the 1800s, celebrities from disparate walks of life—from Abraham Lincoln to showman P.T. Barnum—spoke publicly and eloquently on the subject. They urged their fellow countrymen to exercise moderation in drinking alcohol and to resist the temptation to over-imbibe.[124] Activism of this kind became increasingly necessary in the mid-nineteenth century as German immigrants opened up ever more breweries, exacerbating the situation.[125] It was around this time that temperance societies began to emerge across the country. Men participated in the formation of these societies early on, but women ultimately became the driving forces behind the cause.

By 1873, the time was ripe for definitive action. That winter, a group of Ohio women personally took on their state's saloonkeepers, hotel proprietors and other businessmen who sold various forms of liquor.[126] The Ohio women's enthusiasm was contagious. Other women across the Midwest quickly followed their example, and within a few months, thousands of saloons had closed their doors.[127] Such success was short-lived, as many of these businesses reopened a short while later,[128] but a powerful movement had begun. In late 1874, the National Woman's Christian Temperance Union (WCTU) was born.[129]

Among the WCTU's organizers was Mary Jane Aldrich. An ardent prohibitionist since childhood, she came into her own during the temperance

An Aldrich family portrait, circa 1883. *From left*: John Sr., Carl, John Jr., Luta and Mary Jane. *Private collection.*

crusade that swept the country during that winter of 1873–74. "Quick in thought, fertile in expedients and prompt in action,"[130] Mary Jane possessed exceptional gifts for organization and oratory.[131] She became one of the temperance movement's most influential speakers and tireless workers. Besides helping to co-found the National WCTU, she served as one of the organization's first vice presidents.[132] In 1875, the year before Carl started work at T.M. Sinclair & Co., she became corresponding secretary for the Iowa State WCTU. In 1883, she was elected its president.[133]

Mary Jane performed her professional duties with the wholehearted support of her husband and three children. All of them—but especially her two sons—felt the impact of her temperance work in their lives. During their mother's tenure as Iowa WCTU corresponding secretary, Carl and John Jr. signed the following pledge:*

> *We the undersigned, desirous of becoming if God spare our lives, good*
> *and useful men, and believing good principles and good habits to be the*
> *foundation of good character, because we believe Profanity to be not only*
> *vulgar and ungentlemanly but wicked, the use of Tobacco to be hurtful*

---

* Carl signed on behalf of his brother, who was then three years old.

and useless and the use of intoxicating drinks as a beverage dangerous and wicked resulting in the ruin often times of the souls and bodies of those who use them, do pledge ourselves to abstain from all Profanity, from the use of Tobacco and from all indulgence in intoxicating drinks of any kind for this year of our Lord 1875.[134]

As Mary Jane's reputation grew within temperance circles, so, too, did her son advance in his own chosen line of work. Meatpacking could be a distasteful business and was not for the faint of heart, but Carl rose confidently to the challenge. He steadily climbed the ladder at T.M. Sinclair & Co., gaining experience at almost every level of the industry. From the humble position of office boy, he was promoted to the slightly more exalted one of shipping clerk[135] and to the less savory (and far smellier) one of general overseer of the company's cutting and curing department.[136]

Endowed with a naturally inquisitive mind, Carl soon mastered the business, inside and out. T.M. Sinclair & Co. general superintendent James Macauley substantiated this years later in an 1898 letter of reference:

> *The active interest he has always taken in every work, and in every position which he has been placed, and his determination to master the details of the business, has resulted in his being to day one of the best <u>Posted</u>, and one of the most valued employees of the T.M. Sinclair & Co.'s establishment.*[137]

Family approbation of Carl's diligence supported Macauley's assessment. In 1882, Milton Johnston wrote to his grandson from his New York farm:

> *I have always been anxious and glad to hear from you and have uniformly been well pleased with what I have heard. I have but little knowledge of the packing house business. Whether the course you have gone through and your training there will eventually benefit you in after life I do not regard as material as the fact that you [have] taken a course to gain and retain the confidence of your employers.*[138]

But diligent though Carl was, he was still young—and impatient. The year after receiving his grandfather's letter, he turned twenty-three. He had been working for T.M. Sinclair & Co. for seven years, nearly a third of his life. The passage of time did not escape him, and he was in need of a change—and also eager to revisit his pioneering past.

His chance came from none other than Portus Baxter Weare (1842–1909). Weare, one of Chicago's business tycoons, was something of a midwestern legend.* Like Carl, he had grown up in Cedar Rapids but "while still a mere boy" had "entered upon the adventurous life of a pioneer trader."[139] At the age of twenty, he had formed the Chicago-based P.B. Weare & Co., which handled a variety of enterprises, including the exportation of prairie chickens from the American West to Europe and, later, buffalo robes. Following the near-extinction of bison, Weare then turned his attention to cattle and grain.[140]

Sometime around 1883, Carl left T.M. Sinclair & Co. to work for Weare in Chicago. Weare took the ambitious young man under his wing[141] and, aware of Carl's interest in returning to his roots, offered him the position of assistant superintendent at Nebraska City's first major packinghouse. Operated by Weare's two-year-old Nebraska & Iowa Packing Company,[142] the plant was ideally located in the southwestern part of Nebraska City[143] "on a Burlington & Missouri River Railroad siding on a 40-acre tract donated by local businessmen on South 14th street."[144] According to the Andreas *History*, the pork house was an impressive size: "230 feet by 81, four stories in height."[145] Another contemporary publication described it as "the largest establishment of its kind with two exceptions in the entire West. The capacity of this tremendous establishment is over 2000 hogs a day, and with the exception of two or three months, they have been in continuous operation."[146]

The job seemed as if it had been made to order for Carl.

There was just one difficulty. Weare, although clearly confident of Carl's professional judgment, had misgivings about sending his young protégé to work under the packinghouse's superintendent, a man by the name of J. Collins Lloyd.[147] Weare warned Carl that "Mr. Lloyd was rather an eccentric gentleman and he might or might not get along with him."[148] Carl heeded his employer's words. Weare was ready to sign him for an extended contract,[149] but Carl concluded that it would be best to "come out and ascertain how he liked it" before committing to a long-term arrangement. He consented only to enter into a contract of sixty days' duration.[150] Such prudence would prove to be well warranted.

On his arrival, Carl thirstily drank in the sight of his old hometown (as he would always regard Nebraska City). Nearly twenty years had come and gone since he had left Nebraska—ample time for the landscape to have

---

* Weare's relatives were also affiliated with Chicago's wealthy elite. His sister Martha married Mark Morton, the third son of his good friend J. Sterling Morton. Their daughter Helen would become the wife of William Swift, the son of Carl's future employer packing baron Louis F. Swift.

altered considerably—and his handful of childhood recollections had not prepared him for how developed the town and its environs had become.

Great changes had taken place. Nebraska City was far more densely populated than before—and far lovelier. In 1867, a couple of years after the Aldriches' departure, Nebraska had joined the Union as its thirty-seventh state. Both immigrants and veterans of the recently concluded Civil War had flocked there, keen to take advantage of the Homestead Act. A chain of natural disasters, including the devastating Grasshopper Plague of 1874, had driven away some of these settlers, but many had remained and gone on to help build up early pioneering towns. Prominent among these was Nebraska City, which, due to its prime location on the Missouri River and at a railroad junction, had subsequently burgeoned into a significant industrial center. Balancing out Nebraska City's industrialization was a profusion of beautiful greenery. And for this the town could thank, in large part, one of the Aldriches' early pioneering associates.

Arriving in Nebraska in 1854,[151] Julius Sterling Morton (1832–1902) and his wife, Caroline, had settled in Otoe County the following year.[152] Other local settlers, noting Morton's energy and drive, recognized that he was destined to accomplish great things. (Carl would later recollect his father's own impressions of Morton: "In his opinion, he had the most vitriolic pen of any man of his age, but he also rated him as one of the greatest influences in the territory, helping to bring law and order, and put the territory on a solid foundation for future progress.")[153] Morton more than lived up to his neighbors' expectations. Starting out as editor of the *Nebraska City News*,[154] he quickly rose to prominence within the state. Before the Aldriches left Nebraska, Morton had already served as secretary of the Nebraska Territory[155] and acting governor of Nebraska.[156]

Among Morton's most actively pursued personal interests was agriculture—an interest that would, ultimately, contribute to his 1893 appointment as United States secretary of agriculture under Grover Cleveland. Troubled by his adopted state's relatively treeless landscape, Morton began planting trees across his Nebraska City "ranch" early on.[157] By 1871, he could boast an orchard of one thousand new trees.[158] The following year, he initiated the first statewide observance of Arbor Day.[159] On that day alone, Nebraskans planted over one million trees throughout the state.[160]

By the early 1880s, Otoe County was witnessing the flourishing of the trees that had been planted on that first Arbor Day—and the steady growth of many others that had been planted there since.[161] The result was

J. Sterling Morton (*seated, middle*) outside his Nebraska City ranch, late 1800s. The mature trees are a testament to his early planting efforts. *History Nebraska*.

breathtaking. Published a year before Carl's return to the area, the Andreas *History* supplies a rapturous description of the town and the surrounding region at this time:

> *Its natural advantages are unsurpassed by those of any town upon the river; the site of the city occupying low bluffs and gently inclining planes, which place it far beyond the reach of high water, or the yet more invidious and dangerous malaria; while the eminence is so slight, and in its approach so gradual, as to occasion no inconvenience. Beyond the city, to the north, an undulating prairie country, while everywhere may be seen groves of forest trees planted by the early settlers. Nestling in its valleys and spreading out upon its hills, Nebraska City is truly a city of orchards and gardens, well situated to afford the casual beholder the best possible view of its advantages and its beauties.*[162]

Carl had not come to Nebraska City to sightsee, however, but to work. Creating a jarring contrast to the beauty of the local landscape was the unpleasant situation in which he found himself at the Nebraska & Iowa Packing Company plant.

No details survive to explain the precise circumstances of Carl's abrupt departure—merely a couple of telling anecdotes. Carl chuckled over his experiences in later years as he shared them with the *Nebraska City News*, which in turn reported:

> *Mr. Aldrich was here but a few days when some of the help did not think he had the authority to tell men under him what to do and there was where the rub came in. Mr. Aldrich demonstrated that he could convince otherwise than orally and the disputant was off the platform and Mr. Aldrich maintained his ground.*[163]

As Weare had foretold, Carl clashed with his boss as well. "Mr. Lloyd," the *News* explained, "displayed some of his eccentricity and 'fired' Mr. Aldrich, who by this time had fully satisfied himself that he and Mr. Lloyd could not agree very well."[164]

Carl made the best of the situation. He "took full pay for the sixty days" and treated the remainder of his stay in Nebraska City as an unexpected but much-welcomed vacation. He spent time with "Albert Harmon* and other friends" before returning to Chicago, where a sympathetic "Mr. Weare placed him in one of the other plants."[165]

But Carl did not forget Nebraska City.

Nor was Nebraska City destined to forget him.

---

* Albert was the son of local farmer and orchardist Oliver Harmon and the stepson of Carl's aunt Rebecca Aldrich. Oliver Harmon had been a vice president of the Nebraska State Board of Agriculture but had died several years before Carl's return.

Chapter 3

POLITICS IN PEORIA

C arl was very young when he met his first celebrity—Santa Claus. The association had commenced when the little boy sent Santa "a very inspiring letter, confidentally [*sic*] ordering an array of Christmas cheer that would have driven his father into dismay."[166] Soon after, Mary Jane had taken her son on a "shopping tour," during which Carl found himself face to face with the illustrious man himself who "at that time was doing emergency work in a large department store."[167] Years later, the *Nebraska Daily News-Press* recorded the remarkable exchange that followed, as Carl remembered it:

> *"You certainly are a cute little fellow," said Santa, "and what is your name?"*
> *"Carl Aldrich," was the very polite response.*
> *"And what would you like for Christmas?" continued Mr. S. Claus.*
> *"Aw hell," returned the young man, not so politely, "don't you ever open your mail?"*[168]

It was not Carl's finest hour. It was, however, a herald of things to come. The same ease and confidence that he displayed in interacting with such an eminent personage as Santa Claus would stand him in good stead twenty years later when he began to rub shoulders with some of the most powerful men in America.

Carl's stint with the Nebraska & Iowa Packing Company marked a turning point in his life. If his confidence in his abilities was at all shaken by the experience, it did not show. However, the experience did evidently prompt him to reevaluate the direction in which he wished to take his career. Not long after his return to Chicago, he moved back to Cedar Rapids, where T.M. Sinclair & Co. welcomed him with open arms. Something had changed, however. Carl was "Carl" no longer. Instead, he was known, in a more professional style, by his initials: "C.M." The change was a sign not only of his maturity but also of his readiness—and intention—to make his mark in the world. This he would do, while still a young man, with great success.

It began with a decision that T.M. Sinclair & Co. made shortly after C.M. resumed work for the company. His supervisors, sensing that he required more active occupation to work off his excess energy, promptly sent him "out on the road" as a traveling representative.[169] C.M. spent the next several years crisscrossing the United States for weeks at a time. He covered the Midwest and also journeyed into the South[170] and as far west as California.[171]

But the new job did more than give him an opportunity to travel; it also facilitated his introduction to the young woman who would become his wife.

C.M. had been "on the road" for about a year when, around 1884, business presumably took him to central Illinois. There, in the charming little town of Shelbyville, he made the acquaintance of one of its leading families, the Tacketts.

The Tacketts, originally from Virginia, had first arrived in Illinois's Shelby County in the early 1800s.[172] Colonel John Tackett, the patriarch, had purchased Shelbyville's first hotel, which at the time consisted of nothing more than a "small, single log room."[173] The colonel was in the midst of renovating the hotel when it was honored, in 1833, by a visit from the new vice president of the United States, Martin Van Buren.[174]

The hotel continued to attract noteworthy guests as it expanded into an attractive edifice. During the 1840s and 1850s, one of its regular patrons was an up-and-coming attorney by the name of Abraham Lincoln. Whenever his work for Illinois's Eighth Judicial Circuit took him to Shelbyville, Lincoln would stay at the Tackett Hotel, conveniently located across the street from the county courthouse.[175]

It was during one such visit to Shelbyville that Lincoln formally debated the slavery question with Anthony Thornton, a personal friend of his and one of the town's foremost attorneys. Details of the Lincoln-Thornton debate went unrecorded, but it was generally acknowledged that Lincoln did not cover himself with glory. His three-hour-long speech was not one of his best,[176] and Shelbyville, most of whose citizens had family ties to the South, had a decided Democrat bias.[177]

The Tackett Hotel in Shelbyville, Illinois. *Shelby County Historical and Genealogical Society.*

Present at the courthouse that day in 1856 was a farmer named George Durkee, another friend of Lincoln's and one of the county's "lone rangers" of Republicanism.[178] The Durkees, like the Tacketts, came of pioneering stock. Originally from Vermont, George's grandfather Dr. John Durkee had served as a surgeon in the War of 1812[179] before relocating with his family to Indiana,[180] where he had helped found the first gristmill in Tippecanoe County.[181]

Also attending the debate were two of the late Colonel Tackett's sons: John, a leading Shelbyville businessman,[182] and William Joel,[183] a successful '49er and farmer.

Still a young man at the time of the debate, William Tackett had already led an exceptionally eventful life. Previous years had seen him study at the Missouri Medical College, where he had received instruction from the infamously eccentric, body-snatching Dr. Joseph Nash McDowell, the inspiration for Mark Twain's colorful character of Dr. Robinson in *The Adventures of Tom Sawyer* (1876).[184] William had scarcely started his own medical practice, however, when he caught gold fever in 1849 and journeyed across the continent on foot to seek his fortune in California.[185]

Top: Dr. William Joel Tackett. *Author's collection.*

Bottom: C.M. Aldrich in 1884, during his courtship of May. *Author's collection.*

The venture had turned out well, and William returned home, affluent, several years later.[186] Abandoning the practice of medicine for good, he then set himself up in the mercantile business and pursued the life of a gentleman farmer.[187]

It was also following his return to Shelbyville that William married George Durkee's sister Mary Jane "Jennie."[188] William and Jennie had several children who survived to adulthood. Of these, Corinne May (known simply as May) was the youngest.[189] It was she who caught C.M.'s eye as he became acquainted with the family.

May was well suited to become the wife of an enterprising and ambitious young man. Besides her family's favored standing in Shelbyville, she had received a superior, finishing school–style education at St. Mary's Academic Institute in Terre Haute, Indiana. There she had stood out as an exemplary student who was unafraid of forming and expressing her own opinions and as the editor of the school magazine, *The Aurora*.[190]

In due course, C.M. and May fell in love, and on December 22, 1885, they were married in Shelbyville's Presbyterian church.[191] Following a honeymoon in St. Louis, they settled temporarily at C.M.'s current posting in Galesburg, Illinois.[192] Their household quickly grew until it included three active sons—Glen Tackett (1886), Carl Milton Jr. (1889) and Ralf Johnston (1891)—and, eventually, a daughter, Frances Enfield (1900).[193]

The stabilizing effects of marriage evidently convinced C.M.'s employer that he was ready to take on more responsibility. Sometime between 1887 and 1891, T.M. Sinclair & Co. appointed him manager of its branch packinghouse in Peoria, Illinois. With its position on the Illinois River, situated halfway between St. Louis and Chicago, Peoria at one time challenged Chicago as the state's dominant city. Even with the spread of railroads that won Chicago status as America's "Second City," Peoria continued to be a major thoroughfare for industry—including meatpacking.

May Tackett's birthplace in Shelbyville. *Author's collection.*

C.M. and May around the
time of their marriage in 1885.
Clockwise from top: C.M., May
and May's sister Fannie. *Author's
collection.*

A piece that C.M. contributed to *A Brief History of Peoria* (1896) toward
the end of his long residence there bears witness to the city's position in the
packing world of the 1890s:

> *The Union Stock Yards of this city are far more important in their line than
> the size of our city would indicate. The yards have a daily capacity for
> 5,000 hogs, 3,000 cattle and 2,000 sheep. This is one of the recognized
> live stock markets of the country and its market quotations are posted daily
> in all the commercial centers. The daily receipts of stock will average about
> 2,000 hogs, 500 cattle and 500 sheep. Peoria is a good market for all
> shippers in Central Illinois and receives a large proportion of stock from
> Iowa. It is an important distributing point on eastern business, all of the
> leading packers in the east have buyers located at the yards.*
>
> *An important item in the cattle trade is the fact that about 14,000 cattle
> are now being fed at the Peoria distilleries, but this is less than the usual
> quantity. The usual number being about 22,000 head fed and finished for
> market here. E. Godel & Sons and The Peoria Packing & Provision Co.*

have their slaughter houses and packing houses located at the yards. Both of these firms do a large business in the dressed beef line and in pork packing. The houses are complete in every detail and fully up to the standard of any of the larger houses of the country and furnish employment for a large number of men. The provision business of the city is such that the larger houses, such as Armour Packing Co., Swift & Co. and T.M. Sinclair & Co. of Cedar Rapids, Ia., all have branch houses located here. The location of these branches brings many millions of dollars through the city banks that would otherwise go in other directions. The provision trade has grown enormously in the last ten years and the territory within one hundred miles of Peoria is now almost entirely supplied from Peoria with all goods in this line. Ten years ago this trade was very largely supplied from Chicago.

The packing houses and the branch houses located here all have men on the road working all of central and southern Illinois, western Indiana, Kentucky, northern Missouri and eastern Iowa, and this trade alone will easily amount to about five million dollars annually.[194]

But if T.M. Sinclair & Co. had supposed that the responsibility of a managerial position would encourage C.M. to permanently settle down, it was much mistaken. C.M. attended to his duties at the Peoria packinghouse with his customary diligence, but he channeled his residual energies into political and civic activism.

Precisely when C.M.'s public involvement in this kind of activity began is unclear. Politics had always been of vital concern to his family, and he may have dipped into municipal concerns during his years in Cedar Rapids. However, life on the road had necessarily rendered prolonged participation with any particular program impractical. It was his move to Peoria, then, that offered him his first real opportunity to invest time in causes important to him.

C.M. slid effortlessly into such work. Short of stature and prematurely balding, he nevertheless cut a striking figure. This fact, combined with his easygoing nature, rich sense of humor, gift for oratory, seemingly effortless ability to make friends and professional standing in Peoria's business community, ultimately won him a name at the local, state and even national levels.

His mother's career, too, gave him a model for his activism. During the 1880s, the WCTU's power and influence had spread not only throughout the United States but also abroad. Its rapid growth, however, had been accompanied by internal conflict. From its inception, one of the WCTU's keys to success had been the charismatic leadership of several distinguished women. Significantly, a number of them were from Iowa. Annie Wittenmyer (1827–1900) was the best known of these. A recognized leader in Iowa temperance circles, Wittenmyer was still highly regarded for her Civil War social work when she was elected the National WCTU's first president in 1874.[195] Her leadership, however, was of short duration. After just a few years, a younger woman by the name of Frances Willard (1839–1898) gained control of the organization.[196]

One issue that enabled Willard to wrest votes from the older woman was Wittenmyer's reluctance to incorporate women's suffrage as one of the organization's chief objectives.[197] Wittenmyer, like many of the Iowa women, saw suffrage as a vehicle for the cause of temperance rather than as an end in itself. Willard, a former educator, thought otherwise—as did, it seemed, many other WCTU members.

But that was not all. Willard's interest in temperance had always been slight, at best,[198] and she had a personal agenda that she was eager to further by whatever means necessary. Initiating a "Do Everything" policy early on, Willard remade the WCTU into an organization of her own design—one that existed to further her own pet causes of suffrage and social or labor reform—to the detriment of the original cause of temperance.[199]

Willard deftly cloaked her narcissistic tendencies with winning charm. She easily convinced majorities of WCTU members to continue to vote for her reelection, year after year, and to vote in accordance with her wishes. And yet, over time a growing number of women became skeptical of Willard's agenda, as well as of her high-handed leadership and not infrequent disregard for democratic procedure.

Added to these concerns was a highly disputed question of how the goals of temperance could best be achieved. The Iowa women, whom Willard herself acknowledged as leading the country in temperance work,[200] believed that voluntary organic growth was the best way to ensure prohibition's long-term success. They could offer concrete evidence to prove the practicality of their theory. Prohibition legislation had already begun to spread steadily from community to community, from town to town, from county to county. And in Iowa, it was due in no small part to the ongoing support of the Republican Party that such growth had been achieved.[201]

Willard, however, was impatient. She was convinced that her ends (or rather, those of the organization that she ostensibly served) could best be achieved by allying the WCTU with a political party—one party in particular. During the 1880s, the WCTU voted to formally align itself with the new and untested Prohibition Party.[202] The decision provoked an outcry from those members who believed that, if nothing else, this action infringed on members' individual freedoms—namely, the freedom of one's own political convictions.[203]

Among the loudest protesters were Mary Jane and her good friend Iowa attorney Judith Ellen Foster. By politicizing the WCTU, they pointed out, the organization—and, through it, the cause of temperance—risked alienating the much more influential Republican Party, which had already proved its loyalty to the temperance cause in many states, such as their own Iowa.[204] Far from insisting that the WCTU should align itself with the Republican Party, they argued that the organization should not be affiliated with any political party at all. Instead, each community or state should work with whichever party best supported the work of temperance.[205]

The Iowa women's campaign drew attention from the national press and endorsements from public figures like the Quaker poet John Greenleaf Whittier.[206] Willard, nevertheless, proved intractable. In 1890, a little over fifteen years after the WCTU's founding, Mary Jane assisted Foster in organizing the rival National Non-Partisan WCTU—but not before an enraged Willard initiated a mud-slinging campaign in a desperate attempt to discredit her former friends and colleagues.[207*]

Observing the widespread news coverage of his mother's activities, while also listening to firsthand accounts of her experiences, gave C.M. a veritable crash course in the uglier side of public life. It was a valuable education and one that he was soon able to put to use. Two years after the organization of the National Non-Partisan WCTU, he was elected to his own first known leadership position, one within the Travelers' Protective Association (TPA). Organized in 1882, the TPA served to protect the interests of commercial traveling men across the country.[208] C.M. was just thirty-one years old when he was elected president of its Illinois division in April 1892.[209]

His new role opened up for him a vista of exciting opportunities. In the summer of 1893, shortly after his reelection to Illinois TPA president,[210] Peoria hosted the annual National TPA convention. This included a TPA Day at the Chicago World's Fair, the highlight of which was a speech given by United States vice president Adlai Stevenson.[211] The convention also hosted an event in Peoria at which both Stevenson and Illinois governor John Peter Altgeld were the guests of honor. Several prominent TPA members—

---

* The position of Mary Jane and her Iowa colleagues would ultimately be vindicated. The Prohibition Party was ineffective in facilitating Willard's goals, and after Willard's death in 1898, the National WCTU resumed its original nonpartisan stance.

C.M. among them—delivered brief addresses there on a variety of topics.[212] C.M., naturally enough, spoke on the subject he knew best—meatpacking. The *St. Louis Globe-Democrat* quoted him:

> *I have been putting breakfast bacon at 18¢ a pound, and hams at from 17¢ to 18¢.... What can a man working at $1.50 a day, with a family to take care of, do with meats at such prices. Of course, these were fine grades, but the prices on all kinds are well up. This has been a season of mystery for the pork business. A man with a cleaver and plenty of muscle would have made money. A man with brains who tried to figure out the market would find himself at fault nearly every time. The best experts have been deceived. At the present time pork men are simply feeling their way. Every once in a while those who have got the stuff will put out a little and coax the market. Orders will begin to come in. Business will brighten. The prices will go up a few points, orders will cease coming in, stagnation will ensue. This is the pork business as it is. I don't believe anybody can tell much about it except that in a general way stocks are not heavy, and the hog crop is still light. I don't believe we shall stock up with hogs inside of two years. Here is another thing to bear in mind. Sections of this country which do not produce hogs, but which want hog meat, have been filling up with great rapidity. Take the Puget Sound country, the pine forests of the Northwest, the South. We have got greatly increased consumption in all these sections, and hogs are not raised in them. The high prices are likely to continue for some time to come.*[213]

That summer, C.M. shouldered further responsibility when he became chairman of the TPA's National Legislative Committee. A long-standing controversy had necessitated this committee's organization. For several years, the TPA had been working to secure an amendment to the nation's current interstate commerce law. This amendment would legalize the sale of interchangeable railway tickets, or tickets that purchasers could use over multiple railway lines. It would also permit commercial travelers, who regularly had to transport their company's heavy wares over long distances, more than the usually allotted 150 pounds of free baggage.[214]

America's traveling salesmen (commonly known as drummers) saw such legislation as crucial, particularly where the issue of interchangeable tickets was concerned. (The TPA Legislative Committee was interested in helping to facilitate the procurement of a five-thousand-mile interchangeable railway ticket, specifically.)[215] While on the road for their employers, drummers often received instructions to alter their routes. If the men had already purchased tickets for one destination, they sometimes lacked the necessary funds to purchase a ticket for the new one. Trying to sell their unneeded tickets for money was the most logical course of action, but it was one fraught with complications due to the widespread menace of ticket scalpers and forgers who sold counterfeit tickets to unsuspecting travelers. As a consequence of these "agents'" illegal activities, anyone trying to sell a spare ticket was automatically suspect. An interchangeable ticket presented the ideal solution as it would permit the drummers (along with other train passengers) to travel wherever they needed to go and also to alter their routes with minimal inconvenience and no additional outlay of money.

Anxious to ensure the amendment's passage, C.M. worked persistently to enlist the support of every congressman possible. He wrote to one TPA colleague:

> *Peoria, Ill., Sept. 25, 1893.*
>
> *Mr. N.E. Hughes, President Tennessee Division, Travelers' Protective Association, Memphis, Tenn.:*
>
> *Dear Sir—We inclose you* [a] *memorandum copy of a bill which we have introduced into congress and wish to use every effort to have pushed through this session. We have been very fortunate in securing the services of Mr. Rayner of Maryland, who is very high in administration circles, to introduce the bill for us. When it comes in committee we expect to use every endeavor possible to secure its passage, but we are particularly anxious at this time to bring all information possible to bear on the congressmen from different States, to pave the way for whatever we may think best to bring before the committee. We are satisfied you will do all in your power to help us, and we particularly wish you to write immediately to every congressman in your State calling his attention to the bill and soliciting his hearty co-operation to secure its passage.*
>
> *Would suggest that you include in your letter, also, an inquiry as to their probable attitude toward the bill, and as soon as you have replies from them kindly forward them to the writer. We would be obliged, also, if you would send us a list of your State legislative committee.*
>
> *Any suggestions that you have to offer we will be very grateful to receive. Please give this your immediate attention, as we must act quickly. Yours very truly,*
>
> C.M. ALDRICH,
> *Chairman National Legislative Committee*[216]

By 1894, the TPA's goal appeared close to becoming a reality. Thanks to the efforts of Democrat congressman Isidor Rayner of Maryland, the bill proposing the amendment to the interstate commerce law received a hearing before the U.S. House of Representatives committee on commerce. In April of that year, C.M. journeyed to Washington, D.C., and delivered a personal address to the committee in support of the bill.[217] With that, his work was done—for the time being, at least.

C.M.'s reputation grew as the TPA awaited Congress's decision. A month before his trip to Washington, he had been elected a director of the newly organized Peoria Traveling Men's Republican Club.[218] A few months later, he was elected fifth vice president of the TPA and one of its national directors.[219]

It was also that year that he introduced a new and innovative idea to the TPA. The TPA was not an insurance company, but it did offer its members (or their survivors, depending on the case) certain benefits in the event of accidental injury or death. Problems had evidently arisen in the recent past with regard to ensuring the distribution of these benefits, and C.M., knowing this, came up with an almost foolproof device—metal identification key rings. It was reported:

> *The identification metallic key ring checks will be mailed to each old and each new member on and after October 1, 1894. The check is about the same size as a quarter of a dollar, and on one side is stamped: "If owner is injured wire identification number to address on other side." Then on the opposite side is given the identification number of the member, which is recorded in the national secretary's office, and the address of the national office.*[220]

The proposal proved to be immensely popular.[221] Recognizing that the key rings would provide additional security and attract new members, the TPA (whose membership then numbered around ten thousand) immediately adopted the plan at the TPA Day that was held that fall in St. Louis.[222]

It was early the next year that Congress passed the so-called TPA Bill. C.M. and his colleagues, however, could not claim absolute victory. The issue of the five-thousand-mile interchangeable ticket remained contentious. As the *Chicago Daily Inter Ocean* noted, "The amendment [did] not make it obligatory on the part of the railroads to issue such tickets, but merely [gave] them the right to do so."[223] Most of the railroads, as a matter of fact, were not eager to exercise this right. The *Chicago Tribune*, sympathetic to the drummers' cause, commented on the railroads' fickleness. Previously, the

C.M. during his time with the Illinois TPA. *Author's collection.*

Tribune pointed out, the railroads had argued that the law did not permit them to issue interchangeable tickets,[224] but now, following the passage of legislation that enabled them to do so, they were replete with excuses, insisting that an interchangeable ticket would, among other things, "lead to the misuse of the tickets, the manipulation of coupons, and losses of revenue" to the individual railroad lines.[225]

The drummers, consequently, remained in the unenviable position of having to try to pressure the railroads into offering an interchangeable ticket. They continued to speak publicly in the ticket's defense, even as railway inspectors (the bill's key detractors) continued to complain of potential abuses of the system. The debate was still ongoing when C.M., as chairman of the Board of Trade of Peoria,[226] weighed in with his arguments in January 1897. These were published in the *Pittsburgh Post*:

> *The request for the 5,000-mile-interchangeable-ticket is advanced as a mere straight up and down business proposition. The commercial traveler has opposed a flat rate of 2 cents per mile in the various state legislatures. It is believed that the time has come when mutual concessions between the commercial and railway interests must be made on mutual grounds. It is but fair that the local traffic of the railways, based on 3 cents per mile, should bring its proper proportion of the revenue. It should not be reduced to 2 cents per mile. A study of the interchangeable mileage ticket resolves itself into a simple question as the ability of the association of roads to devise ways and means of issuing such a ticket interchangeably, and surrounding it with the necessary protective measures and proper means, assuring an equitable account as between the roads honoring coupons of such tickets.[227]*

It was in the midst of this demanding activity that C.M.'s political activism took off. Fittingly, it was in Peoria—a city steeped in Republican history, where one of his heroes, Abraham Lincoln, had delivered a speech about the controversial Kansas-Nebraska Act in 1854—that C.M. distinguished himself in the political sphere. C.M., a staunch Republican, had inherited the partisan convictions of his forebears. Both of his parents were committed Republicans, as had been his late great-grandfather Dr. Laurens Hull and grandfather Milton Johnston. Dr. Hull, once a New York state senator, had joined the new party shortly before his death in 1865.[228] Milton Johnston, who had been appointed postmaster of Sidney Plains during William Henry Harrison's Whig administration, had ended his days a Republican as well.[229]

At the executive level, at least, Republicanism had dominated the American political scene for the first twenty-four years of C.M.'s life. Beginning with Lincoln, all of the men elected to the presidency over this period had been Republicans. (The only non-Republican president was Andrew Johnson, who had served out the remainder of Lincoln's second term of office upon the latter's assassination in 1865.) Thus, the victories of Democrat Grover Cleveland in 1884 and 1892 came as a rude awakening to Republicans, who became anxious to reclaim the White House for their own party.

Feelings ran high during the months leading up to the election of 1896. A financial depression, brought on by the Panic of 1893, had resulted in destitution for untold thousands of unemployed Americans.[230] Money, therefore, was a key issue in the debates, which voters followed carefully to determine which candidate would be the most capable of delivering their country from the economic slump.[231]

Running on the Republican ticket was Ohio governor William McKinley. As the framer of the 1890 McKinley high protective tariff bill, he automatically held the confidence of many voters.[232] The opposition, however, put up a strong challenge. Standing against McKinley was a charismatic young attorney from Nebraska named William Jennings Bryan, who enjoyed the backing of not only the Democratic Party but also smaller parties like the Silver Republicans, a defecting faction of the Republican Party.

With both candidates representing the Midwest, states like Illinois took an exceptionally keen interest in the election. One tactic that Republicans in Illinois employed to thwart Bryan's campaign was organizing the Kickapoo Club. C.M., by then recognized as "a power in the politics" of Peoria and influential in the outcome of its mayoral elections,[233] was one of the Kickapoo Club's founding members. Another was a young attorney named Charles Gates Dawes (1865–1951).[234] The Republican Party's choice to manage McKinley's Illinois campaign,[235] Dawes had personal connections that made him ideal for such a responsibility. His father was former Ohio congressman Rufus Dawes, who had served alongside McKinley in the United States House of Representatives in the 1880s.[236] Charles Dawes was

C.M.'s three sons in 1895. *From left*: Ralf, Carl Jr. and Glen. *Author's collection.*

himself personally acquainted with Bryan through his former law practice in Lincoln, Nebraska.[237]

C.M.'s and Dawes's collaboration in the Kickapoo Club evidently enabled them to strike up a friendly and enduring association that was based on mutual respect and shared interests.[238] Despite the economic disparity of their backgrounds (family affluence had allowed Dawes to attend college and law school), the two young men had much in common. Like C.M., Dawes boasted a long American lineage stretching back to the *Mayflower*. Most famous of his ancestors was William Dawes, who, along with Paul Revere, had helped warn the Massachusetts minutemen of the impending arrival of British troops prior to the Battles of Lexington and Concord.[239] Like the Aldriches, too, the Dawes family had been early pioneers in what had once been known as "the West." Specifically, they had helped organize the settlement of Ohio.[240] Beyond this, C.M. and Dawes both enjoyed indulging in artistic expression. Just as C.M. would one day become a prolific (if rather homespun) amateur poet, Dawes would compose the 1910s national hit "Melody in A Major."

The Kickapoo Club's efforts ultimately paid off. McKinley not only carried Illinois but also won the national election in a landslide.[241] His election ushered in a new era of Republican dominance. With the exception of Woodrow Wilson's two terms of office, the Republican Party would retain control of the White House until Franklin Roosevelt's election during the Great Depression, in 1932.[242]

McKinley's victory, as it turned out, was the making of Dawes's political career. He was promptly appointed comptroller of the currency in the United States Treasury.[243] From there, Dawes would go on to fill some of the highest offices in the land. He would serve as United States vice president under Calvin Coolidge[244] and as ambassador to the United Kingdom under Herbert Hoover.[245] In recognition of his efforts to aid Germany's floundering post–World War I economy through his Dawes Plan, he would receive the Nobel Peace Prize in 1925.[246]

Like Dawes, C.M. entertained hopes of an appointment in the McKinley administration. In 1897, the year the new president took office, he applied for a government post in Belfast, Ireland. There, in Ireland, with his connections to the once Belfast-based Sinclair family and their business concerns, he possibly anticipated simultaneously continuing his meatpacking career.[247] But the desired post was not forthcoming. McKinley's government evidently decided that it could do without C.M.'s unique talents.

As it happened, however, T.M. Sinclair & Co. could not. That year, C.M. received a summons from his employer. The company required him at the Cedar Rapids packinghouse. He was to be transferred back to Iowa to manage its sales department.[248]

C.M. greeted the news without enthusiasm. The out-of-state transfer necessitated his resignation from the TPA's National Board of Directors.[249] His blossoming career in civic and political activism, it appeared, was at an end.

The world, however, had not heard the last of him.

CHAPTER 4

TIED TO THE GREAT PACKING MACHINE

Transferring C.M. away from Illinois was the worst decision that T.M. Sinclair & Co. could have made—as the company quickly discovered, to its regret. C.M. had been back in Cedar Rapids for a little over a year when he submitted his letter of resignation.

His motivations for parting ways with his employer are not explicitly documented but can be confidently deduced. One reason was a restructuring of the company that was then taking place[250] and that was apparently disillusioning many T.M. Sinclair & Co. employees.[251] Another factor was the lack of opportunity for professional advancement. After twenty years of loyal service, C.M. was one of T.M. Sinclair & Co.'s highest-paid employees;[252] he had reached the highest rungs of the company ladder and could rise no further. An additional motivator was T.M. Sinclair & Co.'s dwindling prestige. Since the death of T.M. Sinclair over fifteen years earlier, the company had lost standing in the meatpacking world; companies like Swift, Armour and Morris now enjoyed national ascendency.[253] Finally, no personal ties remained to bind C.M. to Cedar Rapids. In 1895, his parents, brother and sister had all moved away to Springfield, Missouri, for the sake of John Aldrich Sr.'s health.[254]

Restlessness also undoubtedly contributed to his decision. Missing his political work and still dispirited by his dashed hopes of a government appointment, he was ready for a fresh challenge. And of fresh challenges, he had his choice. Neither his professional track record nor his highly publicized political activities had escaped the notice of other packing companies. Already some of the biggest of the "big" packers had begun to court him.

The news of C.M.'s decision late in 1898 sent shock waves throughout the company hierarchy. Charles B. Soutter, brother-in-law of the late Thomas McElderry Sinclair and formerly the company's president and general manager,[255] was frankly alarmed. He lost no time in dispatching the following letter:

December 23rd, 98

My dear Carl

Your letter of 19th reached me last night on my arrival from N.Y. I was both surprised and disappointed when I heard in N.Y. that you had arranged to leave us for my expectation was as I told you that some satisfactory arrangement would be made in your case among others.

What do you mean by "the trend of events making it seem best for you to go elsewhere." I wd like a frank explanation of what causes you to think no arrangement could be made.

I would have desired an opportunity to go over the matter with you before it was decided.

It is unnecessary for me to say that personally I am grieved that the change is to be made if it [is] not yet too late to reconsider. Both Mrs. Soutter + myself will welcome the expressions of a personal nature + you may be sure that we return the kind feelings which you express.

As to the debit it wd be a much easier matter if you were remaining with us. I do not clearly remember the circumstances, but I think the amount was divided between TMS & Co. + you at the time. You will please recall the whole affair to me as I must put it before the other partners which I will do. I must close here for train time is up.

Sincerely yours,
Chas. Soutter[256]

No amount of persuasion, however, could sway C.M. He had, it seemed, received an offer that he could not resist—working for the mighty Swift & Company.[257]

The company's founder, Gustavus Franklin Swift (1839–1903), had been a pioneer in the meatpacking business. One of his most important contributions to the industry had been the introduction of refrigerated train cars. This innovation had enabled fresh meat to be shipped across long distances, from the cattle yards of the West to the markets of the East.[258] Swift was equally well known for his frugal ways. Never one to permit waste on even a small scale, he insisted on recycling every part of butchered hogs, using remnants of their carcasses in the manufacture of glue, soap and fertilizers. Such thrifty practices had served him well. By the time C.M. signed on with the company, Swift & Co. was an undisputed leader in the packing world, with plants scattered throughout the American Midwest and distributing houses established all over the world.

C.M.'s first assignment with Swift & Co. was at its plant in East St. Louis,* one of the Midwest's ten most significant stockyard cities.[259] He began work there on the first day of the new year: January 1, 1899. C.M. had barely settled into his new job, though, when circumstances forced him to take a long and very unexpected vacation. Late that summer, the usually hale and hearty C.M. fell gravely ill. As the weeks turned ever chillier and he failed to rally, physicians sent him to the milder, warmer climate of the South to convalesce.

C.M.'s initial destination was a tuberculosis sanatorium in Citronelle, Alabama.[260] There, possibly at the Swift family's personal recommendation, he checked into the Hygeia Hotel, hailed as "the most widely and favorably known hotel between Chicago and the Gulf Coast."[261]

The Hygeia's exquisite setting was enough to send a nature lover like C.M. into raptures. Its fifteen acres were "handsomely laid out in drives and serpentine walks, while beds of semi-tropical flowers, variegated roses and numbers of evergreen flowering trees, such as the magnolia, dogwood, holly and the green bay tree, [were] scattered here and there, greatly beautifying the premises."[262]

But not even the superlative beauty of such surroundings could banish the worries of a once-active invalid. Days—weeks—dragged by without sign of substantial improvement in C.M.'s health. This, along with other troubles, frequently sent him into a state of panic. His staggeringly slow rate of recovery, the welfare of his faraway wife and sons (May was expecting their first child in eight years) and, most particularly, job security—all of these concerns preyed constantly on his mind.

About this last matter, however, he need not have troubled himself. Swift & Co. fully appreciated the worth of its new employee. In fact, subsequent events would suggest that it was already drawing up long-term plans for

---

* The nature of C.M.'s position in St. Louis is not explicitly stated in any known records. However, his past work experience and surviving correspondence suggest that he was manager or supervisor of the packinghouse.

C.M.'s future with the company—plans that would require him to be at his fittest. Louis F. Swift, Gustavus Swift's son and a vice president of Swift & Co.,[263] responded calmly to the anxiety that seeped through the communications C.M. regularly dispatched to Chicago. Far from threatening him with dismissal or accusing him of malingering, both Louis Swift and C.M.'s colleagues in St. Louis urged him to return north only after he made a full recovery:

Dec. 5, '99

Mr. C.M. Aldrich,
*   c/o "The Hygeia,"*
*   Citronelle, Ala.*

Dear Sir: -
*   Acknowledge receipt of your letter of Sept. 1ˢᵗ.*
*   Am very sorry you are not making better headway, but think you should remain in Citronelle until you feel perfectly well. There is no necessity at all for you to hurry back, as matters are going along very well. Our Mr. Johns goes to St. Louis occasionally, and matters are running very smoothly.*

Yours Respectfully,
Louis F. Swift

P.S. A portion of my family will be down to Citronelle before New Years.
*   L.F.S.*[264]

December 21, 1899

Mr. C.M. Aldrich,
*   Hotel Hygeia,*
*   Citronelle, Ala.*

Dear Sir: -
*   Referring to telegraphic correspondence yesterday. Am sorry to learn that you are not recovering as fast as you had hoped, but think that you would be making a great mistake to come back here at this time of year until it was*

fully satisfactory to your physician, and until he considered that it was the proper thing for you to do. I have no doubt that you could get the consent of your physician to return before he really thinks you ought to if you go about it right, but do not think you would be working to the best interests of yourself or of Swift and Company to do this.

Things are coming in very good shape and we are sold up about as close as we can be, and while we would be glad to have you back here when you are well, do not want you to come back until you are in thoroughly good shape.

Mr. Louis F. Swift was here yesterday and this letter is written after talking the matter over with him and meets with his views.

Yours truly,
H.C.S.

Hope you'll be feeling well enough [to] *enjoy your Christmas as much as an Exile may....* [265]

Dec. 23, 1899

Mr. C.M. Aldrich,
c/o. Hygeia Hotel,
Citronelle, Ala.

Dear Mr. Aldrich: -
Your entire office force unite in wishing you a Very Merry Christmas and a Happy New Year. We deeply regret the circumstances that compel you to spend the holidays so far from home, but hope that some of the Christmas happiness and good cheer may be experienced by you in your loneliness. We rejoice in your improved health and anticipate with pleasure your entire recovery and return to the office.

With sincere regards, we are

Yours respectfully,
[Eleven signatures follow] [266]

Louis Swift's tone remained cordial even after C.M.'s convalescence stretched into the New Year and he left Citronelle for Florida's Palm Beach:

Jan. 10, 1900.

Mr. C.M. Aldrich,
Palm Beach Inn,
Palm Beach, Fla.,

Dear Sir: -
Glad to know from your letter of the 7ᵗʰ, that you enjoy the Palm Beach weather, and trust you will not hurry back to St. Louis.
My advices from Citronelle are they are having very warm bright weather and if you return by way of Citronelle you might stop off there a few days, although have no advice to give on the subject.

Yours respectfully,
L.F. Swift

Trade good
All products moving[267]

By the spring of 1900, C.M. was finally back on his feet and back at work in St. Louis—but not for long. A couple of years earlier, Swift & Co. had taken over a small packing plant in South St. Paul, Minnesota.[268] Bent on enlarging the packinghouse to its fullest capacity, the company required an expert who might rise, after a trial period, to the position of manager. C.M. was an obvious choice.

Newly arisen from his sickbed and determined to prove his worth to his employer, C.M. could at first see only the benefits of his St. Paul posting. If nothing else, the pay of manager was undeniably attractive. Within two years of his transfer to Minnesota, the Aldriches were living in St. Paul's Summit Hill neighborhood, home to the city's wealthiest and most elite families.

C.M. had not been in St. Paul long, however, before he came to regret his association with Swift & Co. With a rise in pay also came a commensurate rise in responsibility—and pressure. Furthermore, disturbing developments were taking place in the meatpacking world—trends that were making the work of regional managers like C.M. increasingly demanding and dissatisfying but over which they had limited control. National labor unrest, particularly within the meatpacking industry, was leading to ever more frequent nationwide strikes. In fact, between 1881 and 1905, meatpacking

Frances Aldrich, circa 1904. C.M.'s daughter was born in St. Louis shortly after his return from the South. *Private collection.*

witnessed more strikes than any other American industry.[269] Swift & Co.'s St. Paul branch experienced its share of these during C.M.'s management in the early years of the new century. One notorious strike took place during the summer of 1904 when a majority of its St. Paul employees—six hundred men and women—walked out in solidarity with packinghouse workers across the country.[270]

The crux of the matter, as far as many were concerned, was the apparently insatiable greed of large meatpacking corporations. The year before his death in 1903, Gustavus Swift had joined with rival packing magnates J.O. Armour and Edward Morris* to form the giant National Packing Company, or the "Beef Trust" (as it became popularly known). This merger quickly became a matter of national scandal. That same year, "trust buster" Theodore Roosevelt, who had become president following McKinley's 1901

---

* Edward Morris was also Gustavus Swift's son-in-law.

assassination, initiated legal proceedings against the Beef Trust. The conflict culminated three years later in the 1905 Supreme Court case of *Swift & Co. v. United States*, in which the court ruled against the Beef Trust. This, in turn, would influence the passage of the 1906 Meat Inspection Act and Pure Food and Drug Act, legislation that was designed to raise the level of sanitary practices in food processing.

Also influencing the passage of such legislation was a landmark literary work that was published around this time. In 1904, a young journalist by the name of Upton Sinclair spent several weeks investigating the conditions of Chicago's stockyards. He subsequently turned his research into a serialized novel. On its publication in book form in 1906, Sinclair's *The Jungle* provoked a national outcry as countless Americans were confronted, for the first time, with the unsanitary practices employed within the meatpacking industry, as well as with the exploitation of many of its workers.

Such an accumulation of negative publicity left C.M. feeling demoralized. No one could have been more closely acquainted with the true working conditions of American packing facilities than a thirty-year veteran of the industry like C.M. Unlike Upton Sinclair, who had gleaned most of his material from several brief weeks' investigation in a single city (albeit the most powerful in meatpacking), he had acquired his own extensive knowledge of the business over the course of many years and from a variety of positions and packinghouses. He had, moreover, attained his current position of authority only after working alongside the same kind of unskilled workers the journalist sought to eulogize in his novel.

During his career, C.M. had, furthermore, learned that not all packing company proprietors were greedy, grasping men— and that tragedy could strike any part of the packing hierarchy at any time. In 1881, Thomas McElderry Sinclair, who had built up his Cedar Rapids company by the sweat of his brow,[271] had fallen to his death down an elevator shaft during an inspection of his plant.[272]

Predictably, then, C.M.'s views of the "evils" associated with the packing industry were somewhat different from those held by the outraged American public, which, with a novel

May Aldrich in 1904. *Author's collection.*

as its primary source of information, seemed to condemn the entire industry and its practices out of hand.

C.M. inevitably became disillusioned—not so much with his work but with his employer. The scandals surrounding Swift & Co. had seriously hampered him in the execution of his job at the St. Paul plant. Even worse, the Supreme Court's decision in 1905 gave an impression of damning the packing industry as a whole—and Swift & Co. in particular. To a man like C.M. who had always taken great pride in his work, Swift & Co.'s disgrace represented nothing less than a personal reproach—and a black mark against his good name.

His resignation that spring did not, apparently, take Louis Swift by surprise. Nor did Louis, who had taken over from his father, Gustavus, as company president, appear to go to any great lengths to change C.M.'s mind. He graciously acknowledged C.M.'s decision:

May 17, 1905.

Mr. C.M. Aldrich
   c/o Swift and Company,
      S. St. Paul, Minn.

Dear sir:
   Referring to your letter of resignation will say:
   I accept your resignation effective June 1st. Regret I cannot very well make it an earlier date as I have to consummate some arrangements for your successor.
   At this time allow me to state that our associations have been very pleasant, both socially and in a business way, and that I believe you are fully competent for your new venture, and prophesy only success for you.
   With best wishes, I remain,

Yours respectfully,
L.F. Swift [273]

The "new venture" to which Swift alluded was the position of general manager with a Canadian packing concern.[274] Based in Winnipeg, Manitoba, J.Y. Griffin & Co. was somewhat less well known than the other companies for which C.M. had hitherto worked. Griffin & Co.'s comparative obscurity, however, was part of its attraction. Tucked away in another country and, for all practical purposes, dissociated from any of

America's "big packers," Griffin & Co. offered a fresh start to a somewhat jaded veteran of the industry.

For all that, Griffin & Co. was by no means insignificant. Established in 1880, it prided itself on having been "the first Pork Packing business in the [Canadian] West."[275] By the time C.M. took over its management in 1905, Griffin & Co. had been in operation for over a quarter of a century and was doing a booming business. The main plant was processing one thousand hogs per day,[276] and the company had established branches in British Columbia, Alberta and Ontario.[277]

C.M. had only just arrived in Winnipeg when the local *Tribune* ran a piece about Griffin & Co.'s exhibit at that summer's Winnipeg Industrial Exhibition:

> *Their products are displayed in a most intelligent manner, and the great variety of toothsome things shown speaks loudly for the progressive methods of this firm, who, by the way, are pioneers of the meat packing trade in western Canada; and although they have displayed consistently year after year since Winnipeg's initial fair—their 1905 showing eclipses all their previous efforts. This firm has made such a special study of meat packing that they have passed safely beyond the experimental stage, as the quality of their specially cured "Premier" brand of hams and bacon will suffice. It took years to perfect the process by which these toothsome eatables are cured, but they stand today the only brand of hams and bacon in the world that are cured with an absolutely dry process, without the aid of liquids in any form. This process, says Mr. J.Y. Griffin, gives the meat a firmness that cannot be obtained by any other method, and at the same time imparts a toothsomeness that is unexcelled.*
>
> *A display of Irish rolled bacon, which is a part of this exhibit, is receiving great attention from thousands, but particularly from those who recognized it because of its exactness in every way to the article cured on Erin's green isle. Cooked jellied pork tenderloins, jellied hocks, pickled tongues and many other of the newest productions of the packing trade, are also shown, together with a goodly assortment of the methods of cure found in the London and Liverpool markets.[278]*

C.M., although only newly affiliated with the company, was also interviewed by the paper. Energized by his latest career move, he was more than usually exuberant:

Mr. Aldridge [sic], *the superintendent of the Winnipeg plant…is enthusiastic over the excellence of the Canadian hog. He says that our Canadian grain-fed porker far outstrips his American corn-raised cousin, and resembles more closely the renowned Irish hog than any other in the world.*[279]

In his capacity as manager, C.M. was able to run the Winnipeg plant as if it were his own and as he saw fit. He allowed himself to look forward to many happy and prosperous years with the company.

But Louis Swift, packing baron, had other ideas.

Both in wording and in tone, Louis Swift's acknowledgment of C.M.'s resignation had conveyed an impression of reconciled acceptance. His subsequent actions, however, support a different interpretation.

As early as February 1906, rumors began circulating that Winnipeg's packinghouses were being eyed covetously by "certain Americans"— principally, C.M.'s former employer. The *Winnipeg Tribune* was dismissive:

Many say that certain Americans are interesting themselves in the trade conditions of Manitoba. Though the possibility of another firm coming to the city is canvassed among the retailers, the wholesale houses of the city know nothing more than that the rumor is a hardy annual, and makes periodical appearances in a manner similar to measles.

The manager of Gallagher, Holman, Lafrance & Co., said he doubted the rumor as there were already too many abattoirs in the city, and he did not think another would be erected. As the rumors have been to the effect that Messrs. Swift and company were intending to enter into the Canadian arena, the manager of Messrs. Gallagher was asked on this point, and replied that they are already here. No explanation was vouchsafed.

J.Y. Griffin & Co. know nothing of the rumor, but added that they admired the judgment of the man who did decide to erect another abattoir in this city. Some time ago reports had been published that the Swift Packing Co. had interests in the Griffin company, but Mr. Griffin specifically denied the rumor.[280]

Griffin, it appears, may have been less than forthright in his denials. Mere months later, in June 1906, the *Victoria Daily Times* carried the news of J.Y. Griffin's retirement as company president and of C.M.'s election to the position.[281] An unknown "big American corporation" had absorbed the company.[282] In September, the *Canadian Journal of Commerce* revealed the identity of Griffin & Co.'s new owner: C.M.'s old employer, Swift & Co.[283]

Years later, C.M.'s family explained the circumstances surrounding Swift & Co.'s takeover of the Canadian packinghouse: "They bought the plant without investigation, just because Mr. Aldrich had gone there. They knew that if he were going there, the property was all right."[284]

C.M.'s reaction to the takeover was, under the circumstances, predictable. He exploded.

"I'm through with the big packers," he declared.[285]

"You just stay there," Swift messaged him back.[286]

C.M., however, would not obey.

Under his direction, Griffin & Co. had been modernizing and the Winnipeg packinghouse expanding. A pioneering initiative—shipping cattle directly to Liverpool—had also been undertaken, along with many innovative changes to the plant itself. The *Tribune* kept the public abreast of some of these changes, reporting in September 1906:

> *Many extensions have been added to the plant during the past year. There has been increased freezing capacity and the plant has been modernized in every respect. One of the most novel features was the piling of the river bank to protect the company's property against the encroachments of the river.*[287]

That C.M. derived great satisfaction from the company's accomplishments was evident:

> *"Only a year ago," said Mr. Aldrich, "one could stand on the roof of our premises and survey a broad stretch of prairie sparsely dotted with houses on all sides. Now one can look down on a thriving and bustling community which tells in plain language the sudden though substantial growth of Elmwood or, as it is now called, East Winnipeg. Another evidence of this district's growth is written in the rapidly increasing orders on our firm, these orders coming from East Winnipeg merchants for East Winnipeg consumption. The trade with this district is five times as large as it was a year ago."*[288]

Yet nothing could induce C.M. to work again for Swift & Co. Refusing to once more be the pawn of a large corporation, that fall he tendered his resignation and sold up his shares in Griffin & Co.[289] Swift & Co., apparently accepting his decision as final, appointed the manager of its plant at St. Joseph, Missouri, to take over from him in Winnipeg.[290]

By this time, C.M. had been with Griffin & Co. for just slightly over a year. And a question remained: where to go next?

As one of North America's leading pork-packing experts, C.M. should not have had trouble securing another position. However, his refusal to work for Armour, Morris or any of the other big packers severely restricted his options. As these companies spread their nets ever wider (Supreme Court decisions notwithstanding), independently run packinghouses were becoming increasingly hard to find.

Nevertheless, there were still a few small plants that had withstood pressure from the large corporations. It was to these that C.M. now turned his attention. The name of one, in particular, caught his notice. And before long, his question of "Where to go?" was answered:

Home.

Chapter 5

MANAGER FOR THE MORTONS

By 1907, C.M. was approaching his late forties, and he was feeling the strain of his long altercations with Swift & Co. Thoughts of country living began to hold increasing appeal.

"The Foolish Ones Below," a poem that he clipped from a newspaper around the time he parted ways with Griffin & Co., sheds light on his frame of mind:

In the springtime there comes stealing
Over me a weary feeling,
   And I long to leave the city, with its
      rumbles and its roars;
I possess an earnest longing
To be where no men are thronging,
   To leave trouble far behind me—to be free
      and out of doors.

But I linger where men hurry,
And I toil along and worry
   Like the thousands of my brothers who
      lack strength to break away,
And I look with deepest pity
On those slaves that in the city
   Have so little to reward them and yet
      think that they must stay.

There are rich men all around me
Who have no such cares as hound me,
*   And I wonder if they ever, noticing my*
*   foolishness,*
Speak of me as I am speaking
Of those foolish ones who seeking
*   Daily pittances, are starving the poor*
*   souls that they possess?* [291]

His longing for a simpler life, coupled with his enduring dream of one day returning to the place of his birth, inevitably tugged C.M.'s thoughts toward his old Nebraska hometown.

The timing could not have been better. It just so happened that Nebraska City's sole packing concern, the Morton-Gregson Packing Company, was looking for a new manager.

The Morton-Gregson Co. was a descendant, so to speak, of the Nebraska & Iowa Packing Company for which C.M. had worked so briefly (and disastrously) a quarter century earlier. In 1885, the Nebraska & Iowa Packing Company had been sold to the Nebraska City Packing Company.[292] This company, owned by "a most live and energetic citizen, Mr. Adolph Heller," quickly grew to serve "the entire Union, from Portland, Oregon, to Portland,

Downtown Nebraska City in 1907, the year C.M. moved back to his hometown. *Author's collection.*

Maine, and from Manitoba to Galveston."[293] A rival company, the Trans-Missouri Packing and Provision Company (organized by none other than J. Collins Lloyd, the "eccentric" former manager of the Nebraska & Iowa Packing Company), emerged around the same time,[294] only to soon change hands and be reorganized as the Missouri River Packing Company. Competition between the two packing concerns ultimately ended in a merger. Around the turn of the century, J. Sterling Morton persuaded[295] his sons Joy and Mark,[296] accomplished entrepreneurs, to purchase both the Nebraska City Packing Company and the Missouri River Packing Company. These they then brought under a single banner to form the Morton-Gregson Co.[297] *

C.M. around the time he assumed management of Morton-Gregson Co. *Author's collection.*

Joining the Mortons in their venture was veteran packer William Linaker Gregson, the company's president. Like C.M., the English-born Gregson had begun his career in the industry as an office boy. Once employed by Swift & Co., he had gone on to become vice president of the Chicago Packing and Provision Company[298] and, later, president of the International Packing Company.[299]

Under the supervision of such able businessmen, the Morton-Gregson Co. promised to flourish. A 1902 biographical sketch of Gregson reported that the company "proved a great success from the start."[300] Another contemporary description of Morton-Gregson Co., published in the 1906 *Nebraska City: In Stories and Pictures*, seems to support this brief but glowing assessment of the company's early operations:

> *Main plant located at Nebraska City. Has been in operation since February, 1901. Has one large main five story building 560x120 and large cold storage five stories, size 320x80, besides numerous other buildings, such as ice houses, offices, etc. Capacity 300,000 hogs per year, producing from 40,000,000 to 60,000,000 pounds of product. Employing 250 to 350 persons. Making Nebraska City the second largest packing plant in the state.*

---

* Morton-Gregson Co. was but one of several local Morton family enterprises, prominent among which were the Argo Starch Company and the Overland Theatre.

The Morton-Gregson stockyards exchange office, circa 1910. *Author's collection.*

This plant produces the well known (Coupon*) brand of Hams, Bacon and Lard for domestic trade and the Morton-Gregson Co. brand for export.[301]

More impartial accounts, however, contradict this evaluation. A 1919 report from the United States Federal Trade Commission tells a distinctly different story:

This concern was organized in 1901, with a capital stock of $400,000, but it did not prosper. According to individuals formerly connected with this concern, and who were interviewed by a representative of the commission, the company's lack of success was due partly to poor management and partly to big-packer practices, this latter showing itself in a system of rotation of price-cutting on the part of the big packers in the territory where Morton-Gregson were operating. One week one packer would cut prices to a point at which the independent company could not profitably sell, the next week another would do the same, and so on. Morton-Gregson sold only pork products, but the other packers of course sold beef cuts too, and informants stated that the big packers would sell to the butcher at the cut price only on

---

* J. Sterling Morton was responsible for introducing the name "Coupon" for the Morton-Gregson brand. A 1926 issue of the *National Provisioner* reported that, when urging farmers to raise more hogs at an early Nebraska fair, Morton said, "A good sow is a perennial bond from which farmers could clip their coupons twice a year in the term of pigs."

C.M. (*left*) with Joy Morton at the Chautauqua grounds in 1917. *Author's collection.*

> *condition that he took a quantity of beef cuts at the same time. Thus the profits on the beef offset the loss on the pork.*[302]

Further suggesting a troubled start for the Morton-Gregson Co. is the complete change in leadership that took place several years after its incorporation. In 1907, Joy Morton* replaced Gregson as president of the company,[303] and C.M. Aldrich was hired to take over from Frank L. Burdick,[304] longtime manager of both Morton-Gregson Co. and the earlier Nebraska City packing concerns.[305]

That C.M. had his work cut out for him was clear. But he began his new job that summer with characteristic optimism—and with confidence in his ability to turn around the packinghouse's fortunes. He proved to be well up to the task.

Of greatest value, perhaps, were his exceptional interpersonal skills. While retaining the confidence of company owners and shareholders, he won the trust of Morton-Gregson employees. C.M. identified with them as a fellow "hired man" and took a personal interest in their career advancement. Years later, he revealed:

---

* Joy Morton had already embarked on the very lucrative venture of a Chicago salt distribution company. This is still famous in the twenty-first century as the Morton Salt Company.

I have got a warm place in my heart for the boys in the plant and on the floor. I talked to one boy in our cutting room, a bright, smart appearing young man. He told us he thought he couldn't take the course, and we told him we would help him and do what we could for him.

He made as nice a record in that course as anybody could. Of course, we paid a little attention to him in the way of getting him around and showing him what was what, but today he is on the road and he is making some of the old-timers step along.[306]

C.M.'s approach to business, moreover, was an eminently practical one. He drew on his long years of experience when explaining to his salesmen the importance of achieving good profit margins:

Our competitors, like ourselves, work on narrow margins. They are absolutely obliged to make a profit on their business, and ¼¢ or ½¢ on each pound of product sold means the difference between a profit or a loss.

So that you may be absolutely certain that when you find any of your competitors quoting their product at prices below your own, it simply signifies the discount that the trade insist on their making on the goods which they offer as compared with your own product.

Prices being equal, you doubtless feel that you would obtain the preference on the business. Therefore you must expect your competitor to be compelled

Employees outside the Morton-Gregson stockyards exchange office. *Author's collection.*

to make some discount in order to obtain business as compared to your price. The bigger discount he has to make, the higher compliment to your goods and salesmanship.

The only competitor to fear is the one who obtains a better price than you do, and obtains the business. [307]

To ensure that his messages made an adequately deep impression on the minds of his salesmen, C.M. used time-tested methods—humor and storytelling. He raised laughs in 1926 with the following anecdote:

It happened at a village Sunday School picnic. Two little boys had lemonade stands, one on either side of the entrance.

The pastor came along, and going up to George said, "Well, my man, how much do you charge for your lemonade?"

"Five cents a glass," replied George.

"And how much do you charge?" he asked, turning to Harry, who ran the competing stand.

"Two cents a glass," replied Harry.

The pastor cast a censorious eye upon George and said to Harry, "I'll try a glass of yours, my boy."

As he quaffed the fluid, he smacked his lips and said, "That's good, I'll have another glass," and he smiled when he thought he was getting two glasses at less than George asked for one.

"Tell me, my little man," he said turning to Harry, "how can you afford to sell your lemonade for two cents a glass when George is asking five cents?"

"Well, you see," said Harry, "the cat fell in my pail!"

You will notice [C.M. emphasized] *that the boy who knew his product was all right made no effort to cut his price.* [308]

At the same time, C.M. kept abreast of all the latest scientific and technological developments related to his field. He devoted his own special interest to one particular cause. In the 1920s, he joined the Farm Bureau and Dr. Leunis Van Es, a veterinary surgeon and chairman of the Animal Pathology and Hygiene Department at the University of Nebraska, in establishing a program designed to eliminate bovine tuberculosis. This program would both greatly benefit the meatpacking industry and help guard against the disease's spread to humans. C.M., Dr. Van Es and their associates fought an uphill battle amid "much grumbling" from those less

A Morton-Gregson parade float, early 1900s. *Nebraska City Tourism and Commerce.*

enlightened.[309] In 1928, C.M. was able to announce the success of an incentive program they had initiated:

> *Now that all of the southeastern counties are accredited areas and the counties directly east of us across the river are lined up we receive a very large percentage of accredited hogs; in fact, last week one day out of 2,000 hogs received 1,800 of them were from accredited areas on which we paid the bonus.*
>
> *We are inclined to think that the movement now on foot to have the hogs tattooed in all accredited areas on the farm and shipping points will tend to make both breeders and feeders still more careful and assist in cleaning up and getting rid of the tuberculosis infections.*
>
> *There is still a big loss in killing hogs due to tuberculosis infections and in our case it amounts to 5 or 6 cents per hog on every hog that we kill. At the time this movement was started the average loss per hog was nearer 10 or 11 cents. You can see the improvement that this movement has made in the last couple of years.*
>
> *The most important feature of the whole thing is that we have yet to find a breeder that is not anxious to clean up his place as soon as he receives word that there is a dangerous infection showing up on the animals from his drove, and we believe that by continued cooperation between the breeders and the packers that a very desirable situation will be reached.*[310]

Addressing Americans' ongoing skepticism about the meatpacking industry's integrity—and, most specifically, its sanitary practices—also occupied C.M.'s time. When he assumed management of the Morton-Gregson plant in 1907, the packing world was still reeling from the aftereffects of the Beef Trust scandals and Upton Sinclair's damning exposé of Chicago's stockyards. The decades that followed were a time of great uncertainty for packinghouses as members of a distrustful public shunned red meat.[311] Sinclair's novel *The Jungle* had been out for several years when, in 1910, the Chicago-based meatpacking periodical the *National Provisioner* noted how "public agitation against the meat trade" was adversely affecting meat prices.[312] On the defensive, the *Provisioner* went on to wryly observe how "the last time the sensationalists had to have something to use for the butt of their attacks they picked out the subject of packinghouse methods, and attacked the quality of meat products and the condition of meat plants."[313] There was, the *Provisioner* complained, "no telling when they [might] launch another 'jungle' crusade."[314]

That year, C.M. went out of his way to alleviate some of the public's concerns by giving a personal talk to a consumer's organization. The *Provisioner* applauded his efforts and encouraged others in the meatpacking trade to follow his lead.[315]

C.M. opened his talk by sympathizing with the position of the ordinary householder:

> *To safeguard the food supply of the home and insure the health of the family is the first duty of all good housekeepers, or parents responsible for their children. We inquire carefully as to the purity and wholesomeness of our water supply. We depend upon the efficiency of our national pure food laws as a guarantee that drugs, liquors and ordinary food products are pure as represented, and we recognize the wisdom of the law in a general way.*
>
> *It is the personal side of the matter, however, that should receive our attention. What good is government inspection of food animals and meat products to us as individuals and families? Why is not all meat, sold for food, inspected? What is inspection? To protect people at a point where they are unable to protect themselves is, generally speaking, the object of meat inspection.*[316]

C.M. broke down some of the most commonly misunderstood points of meat inspection for his listeners. He emphasized the advisability of purchasing government-inspected meat—in other words, meat that had

This page: Morton-Gregson employees cutting ice at South Table Creek in 1909. Carl Aldrich Jr. and foreman Joe Tourville are in the foreground of the first photo. *Author's collection*.

Opposite: Employees loading ice into the Morton-Gregson icehouse in 1909. *Author's collection*.

been processed through a certified packing company—instead of meat that was sold, untested for any disease, by neighborhood butchers:

> The preamble of Secretary Wilson's* instructions states, "For the purpose of preventing the use in inter-State or foreign commerce of meat and meat food products which are unsound, unhealthful, unwholesome or otherwise unfit for human food." The government goes to its full limit of authority, as at present recognized, and says, "Where we have the authority, we will safeguard your food."
>
> The recognized right of each State to control the affairs within its borders prevents the inspection from being enforced on those who confine their business to the community or State in which they are located. That is why a local butcher can kill or offer for sale as food an uninspected animal, and the only guarantee the buyer has as to the healthfulness of the animal and sanitary conditions of its handling, is his faith in the ability of the butcher or farmer to detect the disease, and his personal attention to the cleanliness of its handling.
>
> When you buy meat bearing the stamp "Inspected and Passed, Establishment No. —" you have the guarantee of the government itself that that product is sound and wholesome; that it has passed inspection

---

* This was James Wilson, J. Sterling Morton's successor to the position of United States secretary of agriculture. Wilson served in this capacity for three presidents: William McKinley, Theodore Roosevelt and William Howard Taft.

of from four to nine expert inspectors, veterinarians, etc.; that it is healthy and free from contagion or infectious diseases—particularly that dreadful scourge, tuberculosis; that it was handled strictly in compliance with the following regulations: Reg. 11, Sect. 1.—"An antemortem examination and inspection shall be made of all cattle, sheep, swine and goats about to be slaughtered, before they shall be allowed to be killed in official establishments." Reg. 12, Sec. 2.—"A careful inspection shall be made of all animals at the time of slaughter." And hosts of others.[317]

C.M., determined to leave no potential objection unaddressed, was meticulous in detailing the industry's efforts to ensure and maintain prime sanitary conditions:

Animals are condemned as unfit for food for the following diseases: Blackleg, hemorrhage, septicemia, pyemia, vaccine animals, symptoms of rabies, symptoms of tetanus, malignant epizootic catarrh, cholera, tuberculosis (the increase of this latter disease among domestic animals in late years makes it a very grave question), mange or scab in advanced stages, and numerous others, which only skilled veterinarians, drilled to the work, are competent to locate.

Official abattoirs must comply with the following regulations: Suitably lighted, ventilated, and maintained in a sanitary condition; provided with efficient drainage; ceilings, walls, pillars and partitions shall be kept sanitary; all chutes, trucks, trays, racks, tables, saws, knives, etc., shall be thoroughly cleansed before using. Managers must require employes to be cleanly. Persons who handle meat or meat food products are required to keep hands and clothing clean.

The idea is to let only healthy animals be used for foods and compel those selling to provide clean, suitable facilities and clean, competent employes to handle every pound of it, and we have the government put there to watch every detail and see that it is done.

The actual operation is about as follows: When animals are received at the stockyards, before being driven to be killed, the government veterinary inspects them, and all animals showing any symptoms of disease are tagged as suspects and sent over to be killed separately and held for future extermination.

On the killing floors each animal is carefully examined when the heads are removed by an inspector. Another examines the viscera, and if there are any indications of disease, the animal is held in a retaining room, especially provided for that purpose, and reexamined by the veterinary in charge.

C.M. on the job at the Morton-Gregson stockyards exchange office. *Author's collection.*

Once passed by all these men, it is under constant supervision of additional inspectors in all departments through which any part of it passes—the supplies used in curing, all containers, the wearing apparel of the men, the physical condition of employes (no man can work in a packinghouse who has tuberculosis or any loathsome disease), the air in the buildings. No harmful preservatives can be used.

Pure pork sausage could not be so marked if it contained any filler, such as potato flour, corn flour or any beef or meat other than pork. Isn't it worth while getting inspected meats? The labels or names under which it is shipped are supervised by the government inspectors, and if not in line in every detail, shipment will not be permitted.[318]

To conclude his talk, C.M. provided concrete evidence of the meatpacking industry's conscientiousness:

Secretary Wilson's report for the year 1908 shows that at the official establishments over 175,000 animals were condemned entirely; over 108,000 condemned for food, except as lard or tallow, at the time of slaughter and on reinspection; that is, after cured or processed or ready for market were found to be sour, tainted, putrid, unclean, or, if fats, rancid. There were also condemned over 31,000,000 pounds of beef; over 11,000,000 pounds of pork and with mutton, goat, veal, etc., a total of over 43,000,000 pounds. This, at least, looks as if our government inspection is no farce, and should raise the value of everything bearing the stamp "Inspected and Passed."

Bear in mind that the establishments having inspection do not kill much, if any more than half the food animals killed annually in the United States and the other half will probably contain an equal amount of diseased animals. We do not believe the average farmer or butcher competent to protect us in this way, and we believe it is the duty of every community to protect itself by local health regulations on this subject in conformity with the national laws on meat inspection and national pure food laws.[319]

Combating the spread of tuberculosis and educating the public on meat inspection, however, were not C.M.'s primary responsibilities. In addition to keeping a vigilant eye on such far-reaching concerns, he had to contend with complications that were unique to the Morton-Gregson packinghouse. It was possibly unresolved disagreement over how the plant could be most efficiently run and C.M.'s frustration over some of the owners' lack of

The Morton-Gregson packinghouse, mainstay of Nebraska City's economy. *Author's collection.*

expertise, cooperation or even attention to company affairs (Joy Morton's interest in Nebraska City and its concerns was on the wane)[320] that prompted him, along with several other local businessmen, to organize the Otoe Packing Company in 1912.[321] Their plan was to lease the Morton-Gregson plant, enlarge it and make it "even more up-to-date," with the intention of eventually purchasing it outright.[322] The men ultimately had to abandon the scheme, however. Five years later, the Mortons, who owned the controlling interests in Morton-Gregson Co., sold it to the giant Chicago-based Wilson & Co.[323] Wilson & Co., which had similarly bought out C.M.'s old employer T.M. Sinclair & Co. a few years earlier, retained C.M.'s services as manager[324] and vice president.[325]

For the third time in his life, C.M. found himself working for the interests of a big packer. And in this case, there was nothing he could do about it. After spending a lifetime yearning to return to his roots, he had made a decision and would not turn back. He was in Nebraska City to stay.

CHAPTER 6

OH, ARBOR DAY!

The phone rang insistently.
"Hello!" helloed the reporter.
"This is C.M. Aldrich speaking."
"Hello, twice, then," said the reporter.
"Just wanted to say," C.M.A. went on, "that I have flowers blooming in my garden up at Sixteenth and Foist Avenue. If you don't believe it, come up and have a look-see. Snowdrops are blooming in the Aldrich flower bed and praying for a continuation of this bootiful spring weather." [326]

S mall-town living thoroughly suited C.M. His professional commitments necessarily set him a demanding schedule. Besides his day-to-day office duties, he was obliged to routinely break up strikes and also to pay frequent trips to Chicago to confer with Joy Morton and other Morton-Gregson Co. shareholders. His spare hours, however, were his own, and these he passed at a much more leisurely pace. After thirty hectic years, he now had precious time to quite literally stop and smell the roses.

C.M. was a passionate lover of nature (his career in hog-slaughtering and fondness for fishing notwithstanding),* and he reveled in all things

---

* For C.M., fishing was a preferred way to escape the pressures of work. The *Provisioner* reported fishing trips he took to Montana in 1920 and to Yellowstone in 1921. In 1916 (during which time the First World War was being fought in Europe), C.M. wrote to the *Provisioner* from the Colorado Rockies: "Nobody out here cares about the war, U.S. Steel common or the price of September ribs....It's only who has the biggest trout!"

"Gone fishing": C.M. enjoying one of his favorite pastimes. *Private collection.*

living, flora and fauna alike. He had a special affinity for birds. An enthusiastic bird spotter, he would excitedly ring up the Nebraska City paper to report the first robin sighting of the year.[327] He was also their staunch protector. In 1926, when a mass poisoning incident resulted in the unnecessary deaths of a variety of harmless species, he rushed to their aid.

C.M. (*far left*) and friends with their catch at Nipigon, Ontario. *Author's collection.*

The local *Nebraska Daily News-Press* spread word of his impassioned plea on his feathered friends' behalf:

> *Scattering of poisoned grain to dispose of sparrows is also killing valuable song birds, C.M. Aldrich, manager of Morton-Gregson Company, says in a letter to Mayor Thomas.*
>
> *"Is there any law against the spreading of poisoned grain within the city limits?" Mr. Aldrich inquires.*
>
> *"Someone in the past three or four days has spread it in our neighborhood. I found three dead birds in my yard yesterday. Fred Witt found three, Dr. Achenbach, four, and two or three of the neighbors found from one to two lying around their yards. It is an outrageous proceeding. Can anything be done to stop it?"*
>
> *"Possibly you would be justified in making a proclamation against it at any rate. If anyone is anxious to get rid of sparrows that can easily be done by purchasing a trap at a small cost and that will not kill the song birds, turtle doves and other birds that are of benefit in removing bugs, bettles [sic] and other insects.*[328]

The Aldrich house at 1601 First Avenue. C.M. is working in his garden at the left. *Author's collection.*

C.M. was just as passionate about plant life. In 1909, he purchased a large, stately white house[329] at Nebraska City's 1601 First Avenue.[330] On an adjoining lot, he immediately fell to creating an impressive garden. The pains that he took to cultivate his tulips and peonies—and, most particularly, his prize roses—did not go unnoticed. "There is no one in the city," the town paper reported in the early 1920s, "who is a greater lover of flowers and flowering plants than he":[331]

> *He has all about his place flowers and shrubbery and watches and tends them with the care that a mother does her babies. There is something beautiful in the love of flowers and something beautiful in the character and life of one who is a lover of them to the extent that Mr. Aldrich has been all of his life. He and L.F. Jackson are two men in this city who have perhaps more love for the plants that bloom and the cultivation of them than any one, who does it simply because of the love of them to cultivate, to grow and harvest them for others, who enjoy them, but rather prefer that someone else studies and labors with them to reach the results they have attained.[332]*

Every spring, the Aldrich garden was a riot of vibrant color. In time, it came to be regarded as one of Nebraska City's finest.[333] C.M. had been lovingly tending his garden for nearly two decades when the *News-Press* admiringly observed in 1928:

An Aldrich family gathering at 1601 First Avenue. *Author's collection.*

We know positively that C.M. Aldrich is no summer patriot and sunshine soldier, for we saw him at work as late as 6 p.m. 'tother night in his garden, planting rose-bushes, hauling compost (polite name for a substance required for soil fertility) and slapping the ground in the face with a spade. Some men boast of their gardening propensities in barber shops and drug stores. C.M. does his talking with a hoe and a rake. He almost made us ashamed of ourself.[334]

C.M. was generous with his harvests. He made gifts of bouquets to friends and neighbors and also liberally donated flowers to Memorial Day commemorations.[335] When liberties were taken with his plants, however, C.M., who was ordinarily slow to anger, could grow wrathful. Nothing infuriated him more than young "toughs" riding over his lawn[336] or passersby treating themselves to posies from his garden before disrespectfully discarding them moments later. Nor did he waste any time in proclaiming his righteous indignation to the world at large. The *Nebraska City News* took his part in 1915:

C.M. Aldrich is a great lover of flowers and he is not in the least stingy with them, because it always affords him great pleasure to raise them and at the same time give their blossoms to those he knows loves [sic] *and appreciates* [sic] *them. However it does make him exceedingly warm to have people go into his garden and not only steal them, but pull the flowering plant up by the roots. This has happened to him several times of late and he is thinking seriously of making an example of two girls that boldly entered his garden Sunday afternoon and carried off a bunch of not only the flowers, but the entire plants which they went a block away, pulled off the flowers and threw away the plants. This willful destruction of flowering plants, when the flowers could be had for the asking, is enough to make a saint angry and one cannot hardly blame him for wanting to make an example of some of this class.*[337]

Another time, it was dogs that were guilty of destruction. Once again, C.M. vented to the sympathetic *Nebraska City News*, which reported:

C.M. Aldrich had a fine bed of flowers destroyed…at his home by dogs rolling and digging in it. W.H. Penn also had a nice garden patch destroyed by canines. Both gentlemen are exceedingly wroth over the matter and promise to get the dog catcher to get busy ahead of the movement of the

Opposite: An Aldrich rose.
Author's collection.

Right: Arbor Day founder J.
Sterling Morton in 1889. *History
Nebraska*.

*city officials. Both gentlemen contend that dogs running at large are more
destructive to gardens and flowers than chickens.*[338]

C.M. did not stop with the cultivation of his own garden. Rather, he made
it a mission to encourage all Nebraska City residents to try to beautify their
town through natural means. He gave talks to local organizations on the
subject, encouraging their members to garden assiduously and to cultivate
plants that would both grow well in Nebraska's somewhat selective climate
and add to the community's overall aesthetic appearance. "Mr. Aldrich has
traveled extensively," the *News-Press* reported in 1936, "and knew of dozens
of even smaller towns that use every possible means of making their towns
attractive and free from weeds. This is often noticeable for miles before
coming into the place, he stated."[339]

His reasons for prioritizing his town's appearance were, first, to create
the most positive impression possible for first-time visitors to the area
and, second, to ensure that Nebraska City lived up to its reputation as the
"Garden City"—and as the home of Arbor Day. Arbor Day, after all, had
been Nebraska City's chief claim to fame for decades, and it now attracted
scores of tourists every year.

Above: The grounds east of the Arbor Lodge. *History Nebraska.*

Opposite, top: The 1917 Arbor Day parade in downtown Nebraska City. *Author's collection.*

Opposite, bottom: A 1917 Arbor Day parade float featuring a bust of J. Sterling Morton. *History Nebraska.*

Arbor Day's history properly began in January 1872 when J. Sterling Morton delivered his rousing "Fruit Address" to Nebraska's horticultural society.[340] Morton's passion for his subject pulsed through his words:

> *There is beauty in a well ordered orchard which is a "joy forever." It is a blessing to him who plants it, and it perpetuates his name and memory, keeping it fresh as the fruit it bears long after he has ceased to live. There is a comfort in a good orchard, in that it makes the new home more like the "old home in the East," and with its thrifty growth and large luscious fruits, sows contentment in the mind of a family, as the clouds scatter the rain. Orchards are missionaries of culture and refinement. They make the people among whom they grow a better and more thoughtful people. If every farmer in Nebraska will plant out and cultivate an orchard and a*

flower garden, together with a few forest trees, this will become mentally and morally the best agricultural State, the grandest community of producers in the American Union. Children reared among trees and flowers growing up with them will be better, in mind and in heart, than children reared among hogs and cattle. The occupations and surroundings of boys and girls make them, to a great extent, either bad or coarse, or good and gentle.

    If I had the power I would compel every man in the State who had a home of his own, to plant out and cultivate fruit trees.[341]

That same day, Morton proposed a resolution to the State Board of Agriculture, to the effect that April 10, 1872, be set aside and "consecrated" for the purpose of tree planting in Nebraska.[342] His proposal was duly accepted, and his suggestion for the holiday's name—"Arbor Day"—was also adopted.[343]

To encourage participation, Morton recommended making a kind of contest of the holiday. Cash prizes would be awarded to whichever county agricultural society and private citizen planted "properly" the most trees on April 10.[344]

Morton, competitive by nature, undoubtedly had his own eye on the Arbor Day prizes. He ordered eight hundred trees for planting on his own farm. None of the trees arrived by the holiday date,[345] but Morton nonetheless could enjoy the satisfaction of knowing that the first Arbor Day was an unequivocal success. Encouraged by the statewide planting of one million trees on that day,[346] he envisioned that Arbor Day could—or, rather, should—be observed every year.

Morton's vision did not mislead him. In 1874, the Nebraska State Board of Agriculture established Arbor Day as an annual event.[347] Eleven years later, in 1885, Nebraska governor Robert W. Furnas made it a legal state holiday.[348] From that point on, Arbor Day's destiny was sealed as one of Nebraska's most iconic traditions. Arbor Day helped put the state on the map as the idea of a day dedicated to tree-planting spread throughout the rest of the United States.

As for Arbor Day supporters in Nebraska itself, few were more enthusiastic than the son of Morton's old pioneering associates John and Mary Jane Aldrich. Morton had been dead for five years at the time of C.M.'s Nebraska City "homecoming." Arbor Day was still going strong, though, and C.M., recognizing that his town's prosperity was largely tied up in the holiday's continued celebration, was committed to doing his part in its ongoing promotion.

Just how vital C.M.'s contributions were to the yearly festivities becomes readily apparent. Whether it was serving on the organizing committee,[349] taking charge of music arrangements,[350] delivering addresses from the steps of the Morton family's Arbor Lodge mansion, designing a city flag that featured a green tree and the motto "Plant Trees" underneath[351] or acting as messenger between Joy Morton and Nebraska City as the town prepared for the annual celebrations, for nearly thirty years C.M. was as much a part of local Arbor Day tradition as the trees themselves.[352]

As an orator, he found himself in distinct demand. C.M. took just as naturally to the role of speechmaker as he had done in his younger years,

The Arbor Lodge, home of the Morton family, circa 1900. *History Nebraska.*

when he had addressed Congress on behalf of the TPA or exhorted voters to cast their ballots for McKinley. He became a popular speaker not only at local gatherings but also throughout the state. Known as "the silver-tongued orator of Nebraska City,"[353]* he regularly gave speeches at large events held in Lincoln and Omaha.

One of C.M.'s most thoroughly documented speaking engagements is a eulogy that he delivered at the local Elks Lodge's 1918 memorial service. Typical of his style, the speech featured a few lines of verse—in this case, several quoted from Thomas Gray's "Elegy in a Country Churchyard." The *Nebraska City News* conveyed the substance of C.M.'s words:

> *A wise provision of our order contemplates the eulogy of each recurrent year of the virtues of our deceased members and in compliance with this custom we ask you to join with us in spirit as we briefly select from memorie's* [sic] *tablets* [a] *few of their qualities of mind and heart, which linger with us as lasting tributes of their value to this community and a reminder*

---

* Although undoubtedly pleased by such attention, C.M. possibly took exception to his admiring public's choice of appellation, which was so obviously inspired by William Jennings Bryan's own nickname of "the silver-tongued orator of the Platte."

to us of the duties which as men and citizens we owe to our fellow men and the city which we call home. The crowning glory of these men were the simple virtues. Kindliness, fortitude and love of home, though simple, none too common. They were plain earnest men, who did their work, the best they knew how and were kind men who spoke not evil against their neighbors and left no one to nurse the sting of an unkind word. Every day men whose conception of duty was honest, consciencious [sic] performance of their daily task, loyalty to their town, and a religious love of home and children. These are homely traits, but they are the traits that must mark our citizenship if our country is to endure. This order yields to none in its loyalty to country, its adoration of home and all that it implies and can fittingly eulogize these virtues in our departed brothers. Tenderness in them was the companion of fortitude. We all know and will ever remember the brave, patient, heroic way in which each of them picked up his burden of suffering and with knowledge of the inevitable unflinchingly turned his face unto the setting sun, knowing as they entered the twilight zone that sunrise would usher them into a new eternity.

No more for them the blazing hearth shall burn.
Or busy housewife ply her evening care.
No children run to lips their sires return.
Or climb his knees, the evening kiss to share.

There is no bravery in all this world that surpasses the silent fortitude of suffering.
They are gone but not forgotten. Their faults we write upon the sand. And so as in retrospection we consider the lives of these brothers, it is in likeness to the flowers of the summer. The freshness and beauty of youth, the blossom and perfume of manhood. The fruit of knowledge and seed of experience are passed and as with the flowers, each returns to mother earth. We know, that it is not to oblivion, that these lives have not been lived in vain that the lesson of patient gentle kindness and fortitude will be a help to and is a consolation and comfort to those who mourn, even while they cry. Oh, smite us gently, gently God. Teach us to bend and kiss the rod and perfect grow through grief. [354]

C.M.'s podium engagements accumulated every year around Arbor Day. His presence was requested not only at the Arbor Lodge but also in the auditoriums of the public schools. Some words from a 1930 Arbor Day speech that he made to Nebraska City junior high school students survive.

The Arbor Lodge portico. *History Nebraska.*

He began by quoting J. Sterling Morton's words about the holiday: "This is my own idea, the child of my brain. May it prosper."[355] C.M. followed this up with some original observations of his own:

I tell this to illustrate the point…that Mr. Morton had a great idea and wanted it to prosper. Instead of shouting it to the world he worked on it with unselfish motives, helped it grow, until today you see the whole nation honors his thought.

We can be proud of Nebraska City and its connection with Arbor Lodge, not because we can puff up and claim a great man as a home town citizen, but because this man gave the world an idea that was of service. Joy Morton, a son of the founder, also served Nebraska City and the state by giving the lodge to the state to perpetuate the memory of his father.* He has done the same thing in Illinois where he donated 1,000 acres of land as an arboretum.†

J. Sterling Morton offers to you young people…a great example in unselfishness and work.[356]

---

* The Arbor Lodge was donated to the state in 1923.
† Joy Morton established the Morton Arboretum in Illinois in 1922.

Above: The gardens at Arbor Lodge State Historical Park, circa 1930. *History Nebraska*

Opposite: C.M. and his son Glen's wife Esther outside the Arbor Lodge in July 1927. *Author's collection*.

It was through his gifts as a wordsmith that C.M. made his best-remembered contribution to the holiday—the Arbor Day song.

Over time, various people—both Nebraska City residents and tree-planting enthusiasts elsewhere—had come up with poems and songs to commemorate Arbor Day. The less creative had chosen to make use of already well-known nature-related verses. Clergyman and forester Nathaniel Hillyer Eggleston went so far as to outline a "complete programme for Arbor Day observance" that included "readings, recitations, music, and general information."[357] His "programme," the 1893 *Arbor Day Leaves*, featured a wide selection of literature, such as William Cullen Bryant's "A Forest Hymn,"[358] James Russell Lowell's "The Oak"[359] and Longfellow's "Flowers,"[360] as well as songs like Mary A. Heermans's "Tribute to Nature,"[361] Dr. E.P. Waterbury's "Planting the Tree,"[362] J.D. Burrell's "Planting of the Tree"[363] and George

P. Morris and Henry Russell's "Woodman, Spare That Tree."[364] It was not, however, until C.M. wrote his own Arbor Day poem a few years after his return to Nebraska that a single set of verses became a firmly established part of Arbor Day tradition.

It is impossible to pinpoint when C.M. first began writing poetry. He was, by all accounts, "an eager and well-employed reader" who "devoted [himself] to reading a wide choice of subjects."[365] In literary taste, he had long moved on from the highly moralizing and religious poems and stories that his mother had read to him in childhood. Replacing these in his admiration were works of fiction like Jerome K. Jerome's humor-filled novel *Three Men in a Boat* (1889),[366] Henry Van Dyke's *The Other Wise Man* (1895)[367] and—resonating with his own early American ancestry—James Fenimore Cooper's *Leatherstocking Tales*.[368] Supplementing this reading material were more serious selections from New York writer and orator Robert G. Ingersoll and midwestern editor and novelist E.W. Howe.[369]

But it was poetry, rather than prose, to which C.M. naturally gravitated. His personal library of poetry volumes grew steadily over the years until it contained collections by some of the most popular poets of his day, such as Paul Laurence Dunbar, Eugene Field and the "Bard of the Yukon" Robert W. Service.[370] One of the poets C.M. most admired was the English-born "People's Poet" Edgar Guest, whose colloquial, folksy style strongly influenced C.M.'s poetry.

Few extant samples of C.M.'s own attempts at verse predate the Arbor Day song. Two or three poems, such as "My Friend"[*] and "Friendship,"[†] are undated and could, therefore, have been written at any time. Circumstantial evidence, in the form of rhyming correspondence from his friend St. Paul dentist Elmer B. Hause certainly supports the likelihood that C.M. began trying his hand at verse-writing no later than his years in Minnesota.[‡] In any event, C.M. was clearly no stranger to poetry-writing by the time he presented his "Arbor Day" to Nebraska City in 1910.

The song was an instant hit. With a familiar tune—appropriately, "O Tannenbaum" ("O Christmas Tree")—accompanying C.M.'s simple verses, the song seemed comfortably familiar and, at the same time,

---

[*] See page 155.
[†] See page 156.
[‡] Dr. Hause was a fellow poetry enthusiast and fishing fanatic. Following C.M.'s departure from St. Paul in 1905, the two men continued their friendship through correspondence, swapping bits of off-the-cuff verse. Please refer to the appendix for Dr. Hause's "The Northern Lakes Are Calling" and "Dear Milton," pages 179 and 180, respectively.

The entrance drive to the Arbor Lodge. *History Nebraska.*

was easy to remember.* It quickly caught on throughout the state—and beyond. By the time of C.M.'s death over a quarter century later, his Arbor Day song was being sung by "school children and others everywhere."[371] Its popularity would endure beyond his death. A century after he first dedicated it to "our public schools," the song was still being performed every year at the Arbor Lodge.

Arbor Day

The thought that's honored o'er the earth,
    Arbor Day, Oh, Arbor Day.
J. Sterling Morton gave it birth.
    Arbor Day, Oh, Arbor Day.
Nebraska City was his home.
And it is fit that all should come
And join in work so well begun.
    Arbor Day, Oh, Arbor Day.

---

* There is a distinct possibility that C.M. himself first performed the song at the 1910 ceremony. Endowed with a sonorous tenor voice, he frequently sang in men's barbershop quartets.

Come, fling our banner to the breeze,
  Arbor Day, Oh, Arbor Day.
The simple words, plant trees, plant trees,
  Arbor Day, Oh, Arbor Day.
The plains shall blossom as the rose,
'Neath grateful shades we'll find repose.
Though man may die, the tree still grows,
  Arbor Day, Oh, Arbor Day.[372]

CHAPTER 7

A PORK-PACKING POET

The Arbor Day song was just the beginning.

From 1910 onward, Nebraska City witnessed a surge in C.M.'s creativity. The Arbor Day song's popularity was a strong motivator. Encouraged by such success, C.M. began to write more poems and submit them to a variety of periodicals. The result was that he saw one published every year, on average, until his death in 1936.

One of his most reliable publishers was the local newspaper, edited by his friend John Hyde Sweet.[373] C.M. kept the Nebraska City paper busy for years by submitting not only his own poems but also trivia, bits of news or little literary masterpieces that he came across. Sweet paid this compliment to his friend:

> *C.M.A. was my most frequent contributor and in many respects the most helpful. You probably wouldn't know it, but hardly a day passed that Jim Hon, his office helper, didn't drop in with a plain, manila envelope containing comment on a wide variety of subjects. Since anonymity was the rule, I seldom used his name unless, as sometimes happened, a bit of verse or humorous paragraph came from his own pen.[374]*

His own homespun, folksy poems C.M. would drop by with a self-effacing, "Here's my latest bit of doggerel."[375] He was so modest about the merits of his verses that he went so far as to use them as bait to lure autographs from unsuspecting poets. Sweet reported on his friend's ruse in 1929:

He composes a poem, signs it with the poet's name, gets it printed in a newspaper (The N-P sometimes prints 'em) and then sends a marked copy of the paper to the poet concerned, along with a letter asking if he is really the author of the poem.

Promptly, by return mail, C.M.A. gets a white-hot letter from the poet denying that he had written the poem in question. And there, of course, is not only an autograph but the letter accompanying.

Pretty neat little scheme, we calls it! [376]

C.M. and *National Provisioner* editor Paul Aldrich share a joke in Atlantic City. *Author's collection.*

And yet, as Sweet pointed out, C.M. was "too modest in that assumption [about his poetry]. Some of the things he turned out ranked well, were filled with the beauties which always stir the poet's soul."[377]

Another periodical that frequently published C.M.'s "doggerel" was the meatpacking magazine, the *National Provisioner*. The *Provisioner* printed several of his poems, as well as other pieces of his creative writing. These included his "New Year's Menu"* (1916), "Kenyon Bill"† (1919) and "Provision—Profit—Prospect" (1925).‡

Paul Aldrich, editor of the *Provisioner*, regularly livened up the magazine's columns by poking good-natured fun at colleagues through his personal anecdotes and quips. C.M., an acknowledged jokester himself, was a favorite target. A 1917 issue of the *Provisioner* drew attention to his absence at a recent gathering by posing the questions: "Was Carl Aldrich so busy writing pomes that he couldn't get to the meeting? Or was he afraid of losing his shirt-studs again?"[378]

C.M.'s distinctive baldness was regularly subjected to Paul Aldrich's ribbing. The *Provisioner* observed in 1908, "The flies made considerable use of Carl M. Aldrich's polished think tank—every time he moved his hat— as a skating rink. Not a single obstruction there."[379] On another occasion,

---

* See page 161.
† See page 169.
‡ See page 172.

a few years later: "The latest fashion, direct from Hegewisch, is that men must wear clothes to match their hair. D'ye think Carl dast?"[380] And again, in 1914: "Carl Aldrich just had to come. They don't make any better pork packing experts than Carl. It doesn't take hair to make premium goods, so long as the brains are underneath where the hair should have been."[381] Even the solemn occasion of C.M.'s silver wedding anniversary in 1911 could not discourage good-natured teasing:

> *Out in Nebrasky the other day our old pal Carl Aldrich, manager for the Morton-Gregson plant, celebrated with his wife their twenty-fifth wedding anniversary by entertaining a large party of friends at their home. Lots of his Chicago friends would have liked to be there, for there are no flies on Carl, especially on top! They slide off that polished dome, just as easily as trouble slides off the jolly Carl's shoulders.*[382]

C.M. clearly relished his interactions with the *Provisioner*. He responded to such joking with equal good humor. "In reference to the scurrilous allusion in your last issue to my polished dome," he wrote in 1911, "I would suggest that one or two more seasons like the last at figuring profit out of cutting hogs will put a good many porkers in the same class on the hair question with yours truly!"[383]

Grief & Faith

It was not the Arbor Day song's success alone, however, that prompted C.M. to continue spinning verses. His mother's death was another catalyst.

Mary Jane Aldrich's health had been steadily deteriorating for some while when, in 1907 (the same year that C.M. relocated to Nebraska City), his parents gave up their Missouri home and moved back to Sidney Plains, New York.[384] C.M.'s younger brother John Jr., now married and established with his own family in Kansas City, remained behind in the Midwest.[385] Only his sister Luta, unmarried and a semi-invalid, accompanied them. In New York, Mary Jane's condition continued to worsen, and she died in 1909. The

Mary Jane and John Aldrich in their twilight years. *Author's collection.*

event was earth-shattering for her older son, who arrived in New York just in time to bid her a final farewell.

Members of the Aldrich family had long used poetry as a means of expressing their deepest emotions to one another, and they turned now to poetry to give voice to their grief. John Aldrich, who had been devoted to his wife, mourned her intensely. In a final letter to his son, dated six months after Mary Jane's death, he wrote, "I think just as much of my loved ones as ever, especially the <u>dear</u> <u>one</u> up on the hill."[386] He then quoted several lines from "To Mary in Heaven" by Robert Burns (one of C.M.'s favorite poets) in an attempt to convey the pain of his heartbreak:

> *Oh, Mary, dear departed Shade*
> *where is thy place of blissful rest*
> *See'st thou thy lover lowly laid*
> *Hearest thou the groans that rend his breast.* [387]

"I can write no more now," John concluded the letter, "accept this with a Father's love."[388] He died less than three months later. C.M., tied up with business affairs, could not get away to attend the funeral; his wife, May, represented him instead.[389]

C.M. likewise sought solace in poetry. On the day of his mother's passing, he searched out the scrapbook that she had lovingly compiled for him and Luta so many years earlier. Taking the book back to Nebraska with him, he cherished it for the rest of his days. C.M. (described by John Hyde Sweet as "the most prodigious clipper of newspaper and magazine articles Nebraska City ever produced")[390] pasted into its available pages obituaries; other significant family-related announcements; and stories and poems that he happened across and found of special interest.

The first poem that C.M. included in the scrapbook was, fittingly, William Phipps's "My Mother Sleeps":

> *Blow gently, O breeze, in the land of the hills,*
> *Blow gently, and sing ye the song of the rills;*
> *On the slope of the east where the evergreens grow,*
> *My mother sleeps sweet 'neath a mantle of snow.*
>
> *Play lightly around the white stone that is there;*
> *Not whiter that stone than her soft silken hair;*
> *The breath of the morning awakes not to sigh*
> *The sleeper who sleeps in the hills of the sky.*

Rest kindly, O rays of winter-worn sun
Rest light on the mound; the sleeper is done
With care and with toil; the winds do not chill
The sleeper who sleeps on the brow of the hill.

Dear Earth, you must hold her close in your breast;
Hold her and warm the sweet sleeper at rest;
Throw over that mound a mantle of green.
And soft be her sleep 'neath the wealth of its sheen.[391]

In the end, however, C.M. concluded that his mother's memory deserved more than a secondhand tribute. In 1911, two years after Mary Jane's death, he produced "Consolation"* and "My Mother's Death."†

CIVIC INVOLVEMENT & STATE PRIDE

A Hymn to Efficiency

When man arose from out the primal ooze,
With neither brief case, spectacles nor shoes,
To the less recently-created ape,
He wallowed in the mud and was contented
For cost-accounting had not been invented.
Man mounted on the biologic scale,
Lost his prehensile toes and then his tail,
His brain, which was at first infinitesimal,
Learned to work out the points beyond the decimal
And presently, mysteriously and weird,
The expert in efficiency appeared.

With day's first light his industry begins.
He counts the sheets of paper and the pins;
He pussyfoots around and nips out lights;
Upon the backs of envelopes he writes;
To fractional arithmetic he prays
And splits a nickel sixty-seven ways.

---

* See page 159.
† See page 160.

A wasted penny is his greatest crime;
He'll spend a dollar to retrieve a dime—
Not that he needs the dime, you understand,
But to retain his license to command.
At once he saves a penny's worth of loss
And demonstrates his value to the boss—
I would propose for him, if he were here,
Exactly one-eleventh of a cheer.[392]

C.M. "relayed" the above poem to the *News-Press* in 1930.* By this time, he had been managing—with utmost efficiency—Nebraska City's most important industry for nearly a quarter of a century. This meant that he automatically occupied a position of immense importance within the town—a position that helped to inspire his poems "Progress"† (circa 1922) and "Moral"‡ (1927).

C.M., however, was not content to limit his community involvement to purely business affairs. An indefatigable "joiner," he became a member of the Nebraska City Masonic Orders, the Elks Lodge and the Knights of Pythias.[393] At the same time, he assumed numerous leadership roles, becoming the director of the Nebraska City Commercial Club,[394] a principal organizer and director of the Nebraska City Chamber of Commerce,[395] vice president of the Waltonians,[396] president of the Men's Friendly Club,[397] chairman for Otoe County's Republican Party[398] and a director of the Waubonsie Bridge Company.[399]§

C.M. was, in fact, a progressive. Nostalgic though he was about Nebraska's pioneering past, he kept his focus on the future. In a 1925 Omaha speech, he urged "those who love the state" not to "spend too much time looking backward."[400] "'To help the state,' he said, 'Look ahead.'"[401] He led by example. Whenever he heard of a new scheme that might serve his town well, he was the first to introduce it and propose its adoption. Passionate about public health, he was a driving force behind the financing of a local public swimming pool[402] and also the planning and construction of the new St. Mary's Hospital in 1927.[403]

---

* "A Hymn to Efficiency" was published in the humorous "Kick Kolumn" edited by John Hyde Sweet. Although not explicitly stated, C.M. was presumably the poem's author.
† See page 170.
‡ See page 174.
§ This company arranged for the construction of a bridge for vehicular traffic across the Missouri River between Nebraska City and Iowa. The Waubonsie Bridge was completed by 1930.

Top: The Nebraska City Elks Home, circa 1930. *History Nebraska*.

Bottom: The Waubonsie Bridge. *History Nebraska*.

St. Mary's Hospital. *Nebraska City Tourism and Commerce.*

Similarly, he was responsible for importing several new ideas to Nebraska City.[404] C.M. had been in town scarcely a year when he carried out one of his first initiatives—planting near the Morton-Gregson packinghouse an acre of alfalfa, which, at the time, was a "new legume and not yet ready for farm acceptance generally."[405] A Rotarian since his time in Canada, C.M. also organized Nebraska City's own Rotary Club.[406]

John Hyde Sweet bore witness to C.M.'s perseverance in furthering Nebraska City's interests:

> *If anyone were to write a complete account of the Life & Works of Carl M. Aldrich…it would fill many columns.…Moreover, it would be a sort of civic history of this community for the past 30 years. From the very day of the arrival of Mr. Aldrich to assume management of an important industry until the last hours of his life he was closely associated with every important community activity, an originator of many of them, ever an interested and able participant.*
>
> *As one contemplates the diversity of his interests and the time, attention and money he gave to his town and its enterprises, the futility of writing adequately about him becomes apparent. It is as though one were charged with the task of suddenly writing a biography of everybody in the community. One assignment would be no more difficult than the other, particularly when it is remembered that newspapering requires quick report else it is not news.*

Dozens of men have devoted their time to Nebraska City and its affairs, unselfishly, loyally and earnestly. I think it will be admitted that none of these has worked harder nor with greater enthusiasm than the subject of these remarks. He was always interested in his town and its people; nothing grieved him more than to be frustrated in the accomplishment of something which in his opinion we should have.[407]

C.M.'s civic participation spread to include state affairs. A member of the Omaha Chamber of Commerce,[408] the Lincoln Commercial Club[409] and the Lincoln Shrine,[410] he was an active supporter of the Nebraska State Volunteer Firemen's Association as well.[411] In 1928, he was unanimously elected president of the Nebraska Manufacturers' Association.[412] The following year, in 1929, Governor Arthur J. Weaver appointed him as a delegate to the Mississippi Valley Convention at St. Louis.[413] A regent of the Nebraska organization of the Mayflower Society,[414] C.M. was also heavily involved with the Nebraskana Society,[415] the Nebraska State Historical

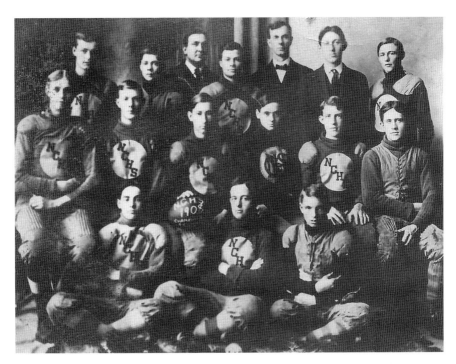

C.M.'s sons Carl Jr. (*front row, center*) and Ralf (*middle row, third from right*) on the Nebraska City High School football team, circa 1908. *Author's collection.*

Society,[416] the Nebraska Territorial Pioneers Association[417] and the Native Sons and Daughters of Nebraska.[418]

It was this love of his "native land" and his passion for public service that shaped some of C.M.'s best-loved poems, including "Nebraska Pioneers"* (1917), "Nebraska"† (1918), "The Golden Rod Highway"‡ (1919), "Nebraska"§ (second version, 1927) and "Stand Up for Otoe County"¶ (1928).

PATRIOTISM

C.M.'s devotion to his town and state was surpassed only by his ardent patriotism. When the United States Congress declared war on Germany in April 1917, he was among the first to begin whipping up prowar sentiment in Nebraska City.

Personal considerations intensified his interest in the war and its outcome. All three of C.M.'s sons—Glen, Carl Jr. and Ralf—served in the United States Armed Forces during the First World War. Glen, a veteran sailor, rejoined the navy and cruised the Mediterranean as part of a convoy patrol. Carl Jr., a former engineering student at the University of Nebraska, remained stateside working on military vehicles at Camp Holabird in Maryland.[419] However, it was the youngest, Ralf, whose war experiences made the deepest impression on C.M.

In June 1917, twenty-six-year-old Ralf set off to join the Norton-Harjes Ambulance Service in France. Ralf, who had studied law at the University of Nebraska and the University of Michigan, had spent the last several years working off and on for Morton-Gregson Co.[420] C.M., anticipating a splendid future for his son, had been preparing him to join an important Chicago packing office.[421] Ralf put his promising career on hold, though, for the sake of "doing his bit." He became Nebraska City's first living, breathing contribution to the war effort.[422]

No one took greater pride in his decision than his father. Before Ralf's departure, C.M. organized a fundraiser at the Morton-Gregson plant, persuading every employee to donate an entire day's wages to the Red Cross, under whose auspices the Norton-Harjes Service would soon come.[423]

---

* See page 162.
† See page 165.
‡ See page 168.
§ See page 173.
¶ See page 176.

Above: C.M. (*center*) with Carl Jr. (*left*) and Ralf (*right*) outside the stockyards exchange office, circa 1910s. Both young men worked for Morton-Gregson Co. *Author's collection*.

Left: Ralf with his father in June 1917, just before he joined the Norton-Harjes Service in France. *Author's collection*.

Ralf's going-away party. *Back row*: C.M., May, their granddaughter Betty and Carl Jr. *Front row*: Carl Jr.'s wife Floy, Ralf and Frances. *Author's collection*.

Ralf remained firmly entrenched in his town's consciousness as his father proudly (and, at first, without his son's knowledge or permission)[424] handed over to the Nebraska City and Lincoln newspapers nearly all of the letters that Ralf sent home from France. These missives from abroad gave Nebraskans a ringside seat to the unfolding drama of the war in Europe. Readers avidly followed Ralf's adventures as he served in the ravaged environs of Noyon;[425] received a personal introduction to his hero, General John J. "Black Jack" Pershing;[426] trained (after joining the regular army) at a world-renowned equestrian school at Saumur;[427] and then headed back to the front for some brief action before the armistice put an end to the fighting in November 1918.[428]

In Nebraska, meanwhile, C.M. did his part to "keep the home fires burning." His most memorable and public involvement in the war effort was a rousing Flag Day speech that he gave in the summer of 1917.

The sentiments that he expressed in his oration may seem naïve in light of the tragedy that was the so-called Great War. Moreover, the shame tactics that C.M. used to urge Otoe County's young men to join up, rather than to "shirk" their patriotic duty as "cowards," come across as somewhat hypocritical considering that neither C.M. himself nor any close member of his family had ever seen combat up to this time. Yet his strongly worded speech is representative of the then-prevailing zeitgeist, exemplifying the kind of patriotic fervor and rhetoric that was sweeping the United States.

The *Nebraska City News* hailed the address as "one of the best ever delivered in this city":[429]

> [C.M. Aldrich] *explained fully the meaning of the word "patriotism," dealing with it from several standpoints. He called special attention to the war in which we are now engaged, and said that each one must do his full part. This is no time for shirkers or slackers. He praised the women for the part they have taken in former wars and spoke of how they always proved their heroism and patriotism, stating they would be found just as loyal now. They were the ones, who, when the men of the country went out to face death before the enemy, suffered the anguish of breaking hearts, but they resolutely faced the inevitable and freely gave up their sons and their husbands that the country might be saved.*
>
> *In the present war one of two things must happen, he said. Either militarism must rule and all the principles this country cherishes be swept away, or the people will rule and the governments be according to the wishes of the people. If Germany is successful in this contest, then this country will be called upon to pay the largest indemnity ever levied upon any one country, and those who refuse to aid now will be taxed such as they never before dreamed of.*
>
> *He spoke of the poor boy, unused to the ways of the world, who knew nothing of war, but who is scared, who is afraid to enlist; and he is the individual we call "slacker." He is not near the contemptible, despicable individual however as he who talks about his great love of country and the patriotic fires that burn within his breast, and then in an hour of distress gives but a mere pittance, when he could well afford to give thousands, declared Mr. Aldrich. He is the worst class of citizen we have today, and all such should be deported to some distant island and made to live alone.*[430]

Posterity must wonder whether C.M. would have been so vehement in his exhortations had he been able to anticipate the lasting harm that war would rain down on his youngest son. Both Glen and Carl Jr. returned home at the war's end unscathed. But Ralf became one of its many casualties. In the fall of 1917, he received a fracture to his skull.[431] While this injury apparently healed satisfactorily, the injuries dealt to his psyche could never be mended. His experiences at the front would leave him suffering from neurasthenia* for the rest of his life.[432] On Ralf's return to the United States in 1919, it became clear that taking up an executive-level position in Chicago was out of the question.

---

* Neurasthenia was a common diagnosis for what later became widely known as "shell shock."

He instead immigrated to Canada, where, in contrast to the glittering career that he and his father had once envisioned for him, he ended up working as manager of the sports section at Chapples Department Store in Fort William, Ontario. Unable to finance the purchase of his own house, he raised his family in the home of his father-in-law,[433] John Rawson Lumby, editor of Fort William's *Daily Times-Journal*.[434]

Ralf Aldrich in uniform. *Author's collection.*

This tragic knowledge still lay very much in the future, however, when C.M. delivered his Flag Day speech. In the months that followed, he turned his attention to other forms of patriotic expression. Inspired by Robert W. Service's *Rhymes of a Red Cross Man** and poems like John McCrae's "In Flanders Fields," Margaret Sangster's "Out There" and William Hershell's "The Service Flag," he produced "The Home Flag"[†] (1917), "American Boys"[‡] (1917), "To One in France"[§] (1918) and "Black Jack's Boys"[¶] (1918).

LOVE & MARRIAGE

Not just Ralf but other members of C.M.'s immediate family influenced his poetry. His wife, in particular, was a source of inspiration. Due to work commitments that kept C.M. late at the office or took him out of town, he and May were frequently separated over the course of their fifty-year marriage. Even after they traded city life for a quieter one in Nebraska City, C.M.'s innumerable obligations robbed them of valuable time together. Nevertheless, he always made sure that May knew he was thinking of her. Whenever business took him from her side on an important anniversary, he made up for his absence by mailing her some affectionate lines of verse. Two of three such poems—"A Birthday Wish"[**] (1922), "My Valentine"[††] (1931)

---

* Robert Service, like Ralf, served as an ambulance driver in France.
† See page 163.
‡ See page 164.
§ See page 166.
¶ See page 167.
** See page 171.
†† See page 177.

and "Roses of You"* (1934)—were among the last he ever wrote.

May Aldrich in middle age. *Private collection.*

May more than merited such thoughtfulness. Her husband's "staunch, good pal" (as he characterized her), she proved herself, time and again, to be a true helpmate. More reserved than the ebullient C.M., May preferred to stay in the background rather than to imitate him by mounting podiums and addressing large audiences. In the time-honored tradition of the loyal wife, she derived satisfaction from taking a personal interest in his hobbies, especially poetry. She was always on hand to help "fill in the blanks"—at times, literally. A friend later recalled this illustrative episode:

> *Carl Aldrich…was presiding at a civic function. He began his address by commenting on the beautiful wording of a famous poem which he said he read frequently and always was inspired by the majesty of its phrasing. After three or four minutes during which he struggled manfully to remember the title, Carl turned to his wife and blurted out: "May, what in tarnation is the name of that poem?"…And May knew: Mr. Kipling's "If."*[435]

Despite her more retiring nature, May was just as public-spirited as her husband. She participated in several organizations, including the Nebraska City chapter of the Daughters of the American Revolution (of which she served as regent)[436] and the by-invitation-only PEO.†

Founded in the mid-1800s as a small sorority at Iowa Wesleyan College, the PEO eventually expanded to become an organization focused on promoting women's interests throughout the world. It was no coincidence that C.M. (who, as the spouse of a PEO member, was regarded as a "BIL," or "brother-in-law" of the society) chose 1927 in which to write his "P.E.O. and B.I.L."‡ That year marked a momentous occasion in the PEO's history. It was then that Virginia Alice Cottey Stockard, founder of Cottey College in Missouri, decided to donate the school to the organization.[437]

---

* See page 178.
† The full name of the PEO has remained a closely guarded secret since the society's founding.
‡ See page 175.

C.M. and May with their daughter Frances (*foreground*) at the Boulder Sanitarium in Colorado, 1922. *Author's collection*.

Family and friends gather at the Aldrich home in 1923 to celebrate Frances Aldrich's marriage to Clyde Parsley. The newlyweds are pictured at center. *Author's collection*.

CHILDREN

The mutual love and support that C.M. and May displayed was not a false façade. Together, they had weathered a series of heartbreaks that they had endeavored to hide from the eyes and ears of an inquisitive and scandal-mongering world.

The greatest burden that they bore together was their oldest son's disreputable career. Glen had been precocious as a child, stunning all who met him with his vivid imagination as well as his unpredictable lines of reasoning. C.M., especially, had taken immense pride in showing off his brilliant little son to friends, relatives and colleagues. Glen, however, had turned out to be a great disappointment. He grew up to be a full-fledged confidence man. As the years went on, his parents became accustomed to hearing from him only when he required money to pay his debts or his father's influence to get him out of impending prison sentences. It became routine practice for C.M. to slip quietly out of town at a moment's notice to come to Glen's aid. Again and again, he gave his son the benefit of the doubt and dug deep into his pockets to give him a fresh start—all to little avail.

C.M. with Betty, his first grandchild. *Author's collection.*

Significantly, it was during these years that C.M. and May were given a second chance at parenting—an opportunity to make up for the mistakes they had made (or felt they had made) in bringing up their firstborn. Compensating them for their grief over Glen was the pride and pleasure that they took in their oldest grandchild and adopted daughter, Betty.

In 1913, Carl Jr.'s first wife, Elsie, died shortly after giving birth to their second daughter.[438] With Carl Jr. unable to care for two small children on his own, the two sets of grandparents divided the girls between them. Elsie's family took the newborn, Mary Jane, while C.M. and May took the older child, Betty, to raise as their own.

Betty effortlessly exceeded the expectations that her grandparents had once cherished for her uncle. A far more sedate child than Glen had been, she

Betty Aldrich. *Author's collection.*

nevertheless possessed an intelligence that was just as keen. An honors student at Nebraska City High School,[139] she went on to graduate from the University of Nebraska with a bachelor of science degree in chemistry. She pursued graduate studies at Northwestern University and worked as a chemist for the Sunkist Corporation before marrying and spending many years in international travel.[440]

As an additional blessing, Betty identified closely with two of her grandfather's most dearly cherished pastimes: poetry and gardening. Growing up in a home where both were found in rich abundance, Betty developed an affinity for them early on. She was just eight years old when— to her grandfather's immense pleasure—her own first poem, "Our Garden," appeared in the Nebraska City paper:

> We have a great big garden,
>   Where pretty roses grow,
> And when it's green in springtime
>   It's a lovely place to go.
>
> So our garden's nice
>   All the year 'round;
> It's even pretty
>   When the snow is on the ground.
>
> And when the catkins from
>   The poplar trees fall down,
> And the tulips put on
>   Her gayest new red gown.
>
> Then the yellow roses,
>   They certainly do stun
> All the people passing by
>   For they're golden as the sun.
>
> Then roses and gladiolas,
>   They quickly come;
> Then some popcorn
>   In the autumn sun.[441]

C.M. delighted not just in his own children and grandchildren, however, but in all young people. His interest in their experiences and aspirations is revealed in his children's poem "Having Fun"* (undated) and in the large quantities of time and money that he donated to advancing the interests of Nebraska City youth. Numerous organizations, such as the Boy Scouts, the YMCA,[442] the Campfire Girls[443] (of which Betty Aldrich was an active member)[444] and 4-H Clubs, benefited from his sponsorship.[445]

His fondness for the younger generation was reciprocated. John Hyde Sweet referred to C.M.'s ability to attract—and hold—the attention of young people in this tongue-in-cheek write-up:

We seriously object to the poetry which is written by C.M. Aldrich. It does not compare, for instance, with those imperishable gems or [sic] *versification which are sprinkled carelessly, as it were, up and down this kolumn of kickosity.[†] But when it comes to telling stories to children, as Mr. Aldrich did Tuesday in his Arbor Day delineation to the kiddies at Arbor Day Lodge, we remove our chapeau and permit our "orban" tresses to flirt with the breeze. In his youth, no doubt, C.M.A. was either a school teacher or a seller of all-day suckers to juveniles. He has a persuasive air that we have always envied—and we do not say "maybe," either. We realize, of course, that he will feel very sorry for our complete lack of appreciation for his verse, but Us Poets are very jealous of our Art. We do envy his ability to hold the attention of a kid. Any man who can do that is entitled to stand before kings or, for that, before queens.[446]*

C.M.'s winning way with young people garnered him frequent invitations to address local school bodies. A single speech—one that he delivered at the Nebraska City High School on Lincoln Day in 1931—survives:

122 years ago today February 12, 1809, two children were born both in God's own image.

One to poverty, privation, hard work and discouraging prospects for education and future position and one with fortune's smile, and as we would say a silver spoon in his mouth.

By totally different paths each carved for himself imperishable, renown and left the world richer and better for having lived.

One was Darwin and the other was Lincoln.

---

* See page 157.
† The Nebraska City paper ran a humorous "Kick Kolumn" for many years.

C.M. and May with their son Ralf's wife, Amy, and grandchildren Jack and Barbara, 1920s. *Author's collection.*

Despite difference in circumstances and surroundings each possessed souls void of offence toward God and man.

It is very fitting that we should honor by thoughtful commemoration, the Birthdays of those whose lives have been a benefaction to the ages in which they lived, and a beacon light and blessing to succeeding generations.

We honor ourselves in honoring them.

Such a life was Abraham Lincoln. A man of the people a man among men.

A man in all parts like as we are—subject to the same emotions, frailties, likes and dislikes, hopes and dispair [sic], passions and human affections, hours of joy and hours of sorrow, feeling as keenly as we the results of failure or of success.

His future from his youth up was the unwritten page; to be written either neatly or blurred by himself as is yours or mine and as is every human being, made in God's image.

On such occasions as this we rob ourselves if we fail to consider seriously those traits, characteristics and principles, the development of which combined to give this immortal character that tremendous influence which swayed the mind and souls of men in his own times, is now, and will continue to be, down the ages a benediction to the oppressed of all mankind.

The outstanding traits of Mr. Lincoln's life were simple, human attributes almost divine in their daily use and application, putting into daily

135

life and service the unselfish philosophy of the Carpenter of Nazareth. He loved his neighbor as himself. The greatest law in life.

He pleased not himself.
He exercised the charity which suffereth long and is kind.
He recompensed no man evil for evil.
He provided things honest in the sight of all men.
He taught loyalty to our Government.
His was the patience which having put his hand to the plow turned not back.
His was the fidelity and application which spared not himself.
His was the trust in the God of nations that believes—
He will hold us in the hollow of His hand and though he slay me yet will I trust him.

He at times felt keenly his isolation and the desertion of former friends, but with unfaltering faith pressed on willing to spend and be spent to benefit his fellow men and save to posterity the Union of States, a Government of undivided people equally free in all their inherent right.

Faithfulness to his principles,
Loyal to his convictions
Patient with the opinions of others,
Kind, merciful and loving in all human relations
Humble before God and man he fulfills the Scripture injunction.
"He that would be great among you let him become the servant of all."

Under conditions which would have prompted many to say "What's the use" he kept his eyes on the goal and pressed on, walking six miles to borrow an English Grammar and reading by candle light the Bible, Pilgrims Progress, Weem's Life of Washington, Shakespeare and Burns, he became the wonderful master of pure simple, concise English which enabled him to express his soul later in that immortal and undying Gettysburg Address, which every student should commit to memory and take to himself that prophetic admonition, "It remains for us"—

Let us, therefore, claim our heritage and work into the fabric of our daily life those traits so outstanding in this character of which the crowning glory is:

"He loved his fellow men"
As I see them they are:
He believed implicitly in God.
The God of Justice, Love and Mercy.
He was unselfish.
He was industrious.
He was kind.
He was patient.
He was persevering.
He was fearless for the right as he saw it.
He was honest in word and deed.
He was dutiful and loving to his parents.[*]
He was merciful to the humble as well as to the mighty.
He was faithful to the end.
He was stern towards injustice and oppression.
He was just and fair.
He was human and had an abiding sense of humor and a heart of pity for all who suffered.
His life was an example of the lines written by Elbert Hubbard: "Let us do our work the best we know how and be kind."

Big in body, mind and heart, he is the best loved memory in our History—an inspiration and safe ideal for all in every walk in life.
Dr. Van Dyke[†] *pictures him closely in his lines.*

Four things a man must learn to do
  If he would make his calling true.
To think without confusion clearly.
  To love his fellowmen sincerely.
To act from honest motives purely.
  To trust in God and Heaven securely.

Let us each in our daily work and conversation strive to our utmost to uphold the sanctity and purity of this Government for which he laid down his life.[447]

---

[*] Handwritten note: "especially his stepmother Nancy Hanks."
[†] This was Henry Van Dyke, author of *The Other Wise Man*, one of C.M.'s favorite books.

CHAPTER 8

ROSES OF MEMORY

Typical of his speeches, the tribute that C.M. paid to Lincoln spoke volumes about his own character—and about the legacy that he himself was destined to leave behind. Just as certainly as his hero "with unfaltering faith pressed on willing to spend and be spent to benefit his fellow men," C.M. sacrificed himself—almost literally—for the sake of his community.

"Am I My Brother's Keeper?" was a question that C.M. once posed to his town at a 1915 Fireman's Banquet. He answered his own question, expressing a belief that "to a certain extent we were" indeed responsible for the well-being of our fellow men.[448] The talk that he proceeded to give reflected his own long and deeply held sense of social responsibility. After addressing (in words reminiscent of his mother's temperance parlance) the ills that the Demon Liquor was wreaking on the lives of his workmen at the Morton-Gregson plant, he turned his attention to the importance of caring for the most vulnerable in any given community. "What Nebraska City needed," he insisted, "as much as anything else was a hospital where the poor could be cared for when sick or injured."[449] He said that "Nebraska City should hang her head in shame because of the lack of hospital facilities."[450] As always, C.M. backed up his words with action. The culmination of his talk—and of many years' endeavor—was the landmark opening of St. Mary's Hospital in 1927.[451]

Just how essential C.M.'s sense of social responsibility was to his community's prosperity became even more meaningfully apparent following the Wall Street stock market crash in 1929. Nebraska City, like every

A 1932 aerial view of C.M.'s beloved hometown. *History Nebraska.*

other American town, could not escape the dismal fallout of the financial catastrophe. Otoe County's vulnerable swelled to alarming numbers. Once-prosperous businesses closed forever. Families who had made Nebraska City their home for generations found themselves with no recourse but to move away in vain hopes of securing employment in far-off, inhospitable cities.

By the time C.M. delivered his Lincoln Day speech in 1931, the reality of the Depression had already seeped deeply into Nebraska City's consciousness. Aware of the bleak future that awaited his young listeners, C.M. took care to lace his eulogy to Lincoln with subtle words of hope and encouragement. He buoyed up the teenagers' spirits by highlighting the disparity between Lincoln's unpromising start in life—his birth to "poverty, privation, hard work and discouraging prospects for education and future position"—and his wonderful achievement in leaving "the world richer and better for having lived."

Not just the future of Nebraska City's youth, though, but the plight of their elders weighed heavily on C.M.'s mind. He felt personally accountable for the welfare of the many men and women he had known for years and who now found themselves at the mercy of the economic downturn—especially after the Morton-Gregson packinghouse shuttered its doors in 1932.

Over the years, the Morton-Gregson plant had ridden out innumerable storms. Its resilience was attributed in large part to C.M.'s expert management. In 1929, the year of the stock market crash, Nebraska celebrated its golden jubilee. The Morton-Gregson Co. took this opportunity to honor C.M., a man (it was said) "whose vision, good judgment and humanitarianism [had] been responsible in no small degree for the large measure of success that [had] come to this company in recent years."[452] Earlier, the sales department had dispatched letters "bearing at the top the likeness of Mr. Aldrich" to all of the company's salesmen.[453] These letters "set forth the aim of the department" to "sell during the week a greater tonnage of meat than the company had ever before sold in the same length of time."[454] Some months later, the Morton-Gregson Co. paid C.M. another tribute by proclaiming "Aldrich week."[455] Plant employees outdid themselves to make their manager proud. The company's car route department reported that it wrote "more orders than ever were written for a like period in the history of the company."[456] At the same time, the company sold a "straight carload of Wilson* canned foods," which "put 25,206 pieces of advertising on dealers' shelves."[457]

By this time, the plant had undergone considerable changes. Notably, a strike in 1922 had resulted in alterations to its government. The workers had organized their own system, which included "a Joint Representative Committee of eight men, four elected from the various departments in the plant and four appointed by the company. In addition there [were] an impartial chairman and secretary who [had] no voting powers on the committee."[458] C.M. alluded favorably to this arrangement ten years later:

> *They consider questions of working conditions themselves.....No contribution list of any kind goes through the plant without the approval of the committee. If there are any labor questions the committee discusses them and agrees upon matters of policy. If an employe's conduct is questioned his case goes before the committee.*[459]

The next stop after the committee was the packinghouse superintendent and the manager (that is, C.M.). If these two men failed to give satisfaction, then the company owner himself, Thomas Wilson, could be appealed to.[460]

By 1932, the Morton-Gregson plant was employing approximately four hundred men and women. Of these, 60 percent were said to be men with

---

* Following Wilson & Co.'s 1917 takeover of Morton-Gregson Co., the packinghouse and its products were officially identified with the Wilson name.

families; 40 percent to be local homeowners; and 65 percent to be married and "supporting homes."[461] Interviewed by the *News-Press*, C.M. had nothing but praise for them. He remarked:

> *Our employes…are sober, industrious and loyal citizens. Many whole families work in our plant, and since I have been here I have seen entire families grow up in our employ.…Our employes are the class of people that you meet on the streets, in the stores, in church.…They are loyal citizens as far as Nebraska City goes. They are generous, too.*[462]

He also took advantage of the opportunity to emphasize the importance of buying local. Alluding to a mutual benefit association and a voluntary relief fund that Morton-Gregson employees had set up the year before, he urged:

> *People of Nebraska City should take that into consideration when they buy their meat. Many people do not stop to think what a vital thing to the community this packing plant is. They don't stop to think what it would mean if all the Morton-Gregson company employes were out of work.*[463]

A bleak view of the Nebraska City packing plant exterior in 1935. *History Nebraska.*

This page and opposite: Nebraska City packing plant employees at work in 1935. *History Nebraska.*

That Morton-Gregson employees could soon be out of work was an all too distressingly real possibility—and one that became a reality mere months after C.M.'s interview with the *News-Press*. In the summer of 1932, the packinghouse ceased operations—without any guarantee of ever starting them up again.[464]

The plant's closure spelled disaster for Nebraska City, sparking an unprecedented diaspora of local residents—and all but shattering the plant's faithful manager in the process. C.M. was forced to stand by and watch "his own house of dreams" (as one friend described it) "pass into thin air."[465]

He did not, however, give up on the packinghouse. Nor did he turn his back on Nebraska City. C.M. continued to take an active role in municipal affairs, all the while lobbying energetically for the plant's reopening. His efforts met with success. In August 1933, the packinghouse reopened under the Federal Emergency Relief Administration.[466] Thomas Wilson had turned over the packinghouse to the federal government "for one year without charge."[467] But that was not all. Wilson had, furthermore, "offered the government the services, also without charge, of the local Morton-Gregson company manager," who thus became "a virtual $1 a year man in the employ of the government."[468]

The worst was not yet over, though. Less than half a year after the reopening, the company's livestock exchange building burned to the ground. The blaze was so spectacular that it could be seen as far as Lincoln, forty miles away.[469] C.M. estimated the damage at approximately $30,000.[470] Also lost was some of his own property—"personal effects collected by him over a period of 40 years."[471]

Discouraged but undaunted, he carried on as before, managing the plant with utmost efficiency and letting all other concerns fall by the wayside as he strove to get his town's economy back on its feet. Such dedication, however, came with a price.

Now in his mid-seventies, C.M. was still one of the pork-packing industry's most respected authorities.[472] He had been working as a packer for nearly sixty years when, in 1935, a colleague observed, "A long line of famous names in the industry were C.M.'s associates during his years of service, and he alone remains still active in the harness, a famous trainer of men and beloved by all who have been associated with him."[473]

Appearances, however, were deceptive. While C.M. outwardly gave an impression of still thriving "in the harness," the reality was quite different. The steady mounting of his responsibilities over time, combined with a series of unforeseeable professional and personal calamities, had taken a devastating toll on his health.

The plant had been open again for only two years when, in late 1935, C.M. collapsed on his way to work. The *News-Press* later reported: "On a morning when the snow was particularly deep he fell exhausted near his office…outside Nebraska City after he had walked from the highway, where he left his taxi, through the drifts. Employes carried him to the office."[474] C.M., concerned about what action the government might take if it heard of his infirmity, swore the men to secrecy.[475]

From then on, as far as he was concerned, it was business as usual. His outlook that winter was, in fact, more than characteristically cheerful. In December, he and May celebrated their golden wedding anniversary—an occasion that was made doubly precious by the knowledge that they would become great-grandparents for the first time the following summer. Adding to C.M.'s content was his peace of mind about his oldest son. Glen, whose criminal activities had culminated in a prison sentence, had been paroled to his father's custody in 1932, the summer of the Morton-Gregson plant's closing. Now, for the first time in years, he was living quietly and respectably at home with his parents.

C.M., however, was fading fast.

Spring came late in 1936. On March 28, the first flowers of the season— four yellow tulips, blooming a week behind schedule—were sighted in C.M.'s garden.[476] Two weeks later, C.M. died in his sleep from a heart attack. The *News-Press* related the circumstances of his passing on April 13:

> *He had not been seriously ill. Sunday a doctor was called to his home, 1601 First avenue, and he was ordered to bed to rest for perhaps a few days. Early in the afternoon he sat in his room reading, then went to bed upon the advice of his physician, making plans to superintend Monday from his upstairs window the uncovering of the roses he so loved. He was particularly pleased because his flowers were spared by the severe winter.*[477]

His son stayed up with him:

> *Glen talked to his father at 1 a.m. Monday in his bedroom. He wasn't feeling particularly unwell and didn't care about being forced to stay in bed.*
>
> *"Turn out the light and get out," Mr. Aldrich laughed after he and his son made plans for the ceremony of uncovering the flowers Monday. These were his last words.*
>
> *At 6:30 a.m. Glen went to his father's room, found him just as he had gone to sleep five or six hours before, his arm over his face as he was accustomed to sleeping, the bed clothing unrumpled.*[478]

C.M. with May in 1935, the year before his death. *Author's collection.*

C.M., it was discovered, had not taken his physician's advice seriously. He had allowed business matters to continue to preoccupy his mind, even to the very last. May Aldrich later found a piece of note paper on which he had scribbled:

> *4-11-36*
>
> *Memo. of agreement between W.M. Wolfe and Morton Gregson Co giving Mr. Wolf [use] of the Pasture South of W.H. Enclosure & East of Old Office site about 3 or 4 acres. Wolf to maintain fences to keep reasonably free of weeds—*
> *Rental for Season $20.00 payable 5.00 monthly at least commencing April 1936.*
>
>

Morton Gregson Co
CM Aldrich[479]

Word of C.M.'s passing swiftly spread throughout the Midwest as the *Chicago Tribune* and other periodicals carried the news. Friends, family and former neighbors hurried to Nebraska City to pay their respects to "a real Christian, a splendid friend and everything a good man could be."[480] C.M.'s funeral on April 15 was held at St. Mary's Episcopal Church, where he had been serving as senior warden.[481] The Knights Templar conducted the graveside service later that day in Wyuka Cemetery.[482]

Nebraska City did not quickly recover from the shock of C.M.'s death. Over the coming weeks and months, the town staggered under the impact. For nearly thirty years, its fate had been inextricably linked with his own, and trying to contemplate a future of which he was not a part, either as manager of the city's major industry or as a tireless champion of local causes, was disorienting. His friend John W. Steinhart reflected on the tremendous effect that C.M. had had on their community:

> *The death of Carl M. Aldrich is a distinct shock to me. I so well recall the days of his arrival at Nebraska City with his family and the announcement that he was going to take over the management of the Morton-Gregson Company. What a wonderful job he did, how the packing plant broadened out and became such a wonderful asset to our city and over and above the industrial side, consider Carl M. Aldrich as a citizen, so active, so interested, so helpful along every community line of activity. I count his life as a benediction to our city and we may well grieve and sorrow over his passing.*

St. Mary's Episcopal Church. C.M. was senior warden there at the time of his death.
Morton-James Public Library, Main Street Historians Collection, Nebraska City, NE.

> *Citizenship is a real, a constructive responsibility, and Carl M. Aldrich's*
> *record is 100% and over, along every possible line.*[483]

Other friends honored his memory through various forms of tribute—including poetry. The Reverend Fletcher Marion Sisson was one who chose verse to celebrate C.M.'s life. Sisson, a retired Methodist minister,[484] was a writer himself and the author of the books *Shepherd's Staff* and *Wooden Shoes or the Worth of the Common Man.*[485] He presented C.M.'s widow with a free verse poem titled "He Called Me 'Buddy'":

> *A manly man has left us,*
> *The charm of C.M. Aldrich is gone,*
> *But his influence remains.*
> *He loved people because they were men:*
> *Not what they were or what they possessed*
> *But because of that some thing in all*
> *That bore the image of their Creator.*
> *The rich and the poor, the high and low,*
> *To him were all the same.*

The men on the street, stores or bank,
In sunshine or rain, all were one to him.
People every where responded to his good cheer.
In home or abroad, in church or state
He had a place and a charm,
Always commanding attention and respect.
His nature was spiritual and all were bettered by it.
He saw God in everything,
Especially in the fragrance and beauty of flowers.
With you I loved him, and we all will miss him.[486]

Through poetry, too, homage was paid to one of C.M.'s greatest passions. Nebraska City observed Arbor Day less than two weeks after his death.[487] His involvement in the holiday's celebration was not forgotten—nor was his affinity for growing, living things. Florence Rice, a neighbor and flower lover who had frequently been a recipient of beautiful rose bouquets from the Aldrich garden, recalled his generosity as she witnessed the gorgeous blooming of his flowers that spring. She wrote the nostalgic "Roses of Memory":

They bloom in his garden,
Where he gave them tender care.
Their pure dainty fragrance,
Sweetly perfumes the air.

Their fresh, dewy petals
Gave him greeting each morn,
As he plucked the lovely blossoms
A friend's home to adorn.

He loved them for their color,
And for the joy they gave,
As he shared his choicest roses,
—Very few did he save.

The sun and rain helped him
To make these flowers grow,
But his ever faithful labor
Only his loved ones know.

The interior of St. Mary's Episcopal Church decorated for C.M.'s memorial service. *Author's collection.*

Always in his garden
Roses of memory will grow,
And always the hearts of friends
This sweet memory will know.

They bloom in his garden
Where he gave them tender care,
Still he walks among them,
His presence,—always there.[488]

It was the testimony of C.M.'s friend John Hyde Sweet, however, that most poignantly summed up the rich legacy that he left behind:

As business man, civic-minded citizen and "family man," Carl Aldrich possessed those traits of character we call admirable. As a close friend said yesterday, his life was indeed a benediction. It is well that we do not forget *the unselfish and devoted service he rendered. He loved all that was beautiful and good, from the rose-garden which was his hobby to the literature of the ages. One may say of him without exaggeration, as a noted American* declaimed over the body of his brother "He believed that happiness was the only good, reason the only torch, justice the only worship, humanity the only religion, and love the only priest. He added to the sum of human joy; and were every one to whom he did a loving service to bring a blossom to his grave, he would sleep tonight beneath a wilderness of flowers."*[489]

---

* This was Robert G. Ingersoll, one of C.M.'s favorite writers.

PART II

The Poems

MY FRIEND

(undated)

The Storms may come,
The cold winds blow,
Still am I blest
For this I know:

My friend's my friend
While life shall last,
Till care shall cease
And time be past.

This is my friend
That I call true—
This friend, my friend
I know is you—"just you."

FRIENDSHIP

(*UNDATED*)

Care and the years
   My form may bend;
Still am I blest,
   I have a friend.

This friend, my friend,
   Is staunch and true.
This friend, my friend,
   Is simply you.

HAVING FUN

(undated)

Hey—Baby! Say—Baby! Baby, where are you?
Now where's my little baby? Where—oh, peek-a-boo!
Now who would e'er have thought it, thought that two hands so wee
Could hide a baby big as you, out of the sight of me?

I looked beneath the chiffonier, I looked behind the door,
I looked into the closet dark, then stretched out on the floor.
I looked beneath the bed for you; then heard your laughter chime,
And there you were behind your hands, a-hiding all the time.

I ran out in the hallway and searched beneath the chairs;
I shook the long portiere for you and galloped down the stairs;
Who would have thought the wee pink lids that close the eyes of you
Could hide a baby from her dad—I see you! Peek-a-boo!

ARBOR DAY

"dedicated to our public schools"

1910

Tune: "My Maryland" or "O Tannenbaum"

The thought that's honored o'er the earth,
    Arbor Day, Oh, Arbor Day.
J. Sterling Morton gave it birth.
    Arbor Day, Oh, Arbor Day.
Nebraska City was his home.
And it is fit that all should come
And join in work so well begun.
    Arbor Day, Oh, Arbor Day.

Come, fling our banner to the breeze,
    Arbor Day, Oh, Arbor Day.
The simple words, plant trees, plant trees,
    Arbor Day, Oh, Arbor Day.
The plains shall blossom as the rose,
'Neath grateful shades we'll find repose,
Though man may die, the tree still grows,
    Arbor Day, Oh, Arbor Day.

CONSOLATION

APRIL 5, 1911

Oh, that my Mother's constant faith
   And loving trust in God
Might heal my bruised heart while I kneel
   And mutely kiss the rod.

The loving heart that trusted on
   Even though his hand should slay,
And through the darkness and the night
   Looked to the perfect Day.

The weary days drag plodding on;
   But to my anxious soul
Her trusting voice still sweetly sings,
   "Thy God shall make thee whole."

MY MOTHER'S DEATH

1911

The long, dread night drew to a close,
The gray dawn spoke the coming day;
A gasp, a tremor, and the soul
Burst from its tenement of clay.
The wasted body racked so long
From mortal pain at last is free.
The sweet face, with a peaceful smile,
Greets the new dawn, Eternity.

Oh, could that Mother's strong, clear faith,
A legacy with me abide;
Then could I say, "Thy will be done,"
And, trusting, smile whate'er betide.
Though he should slay, yet would I trust,
That loving heart, my Mother's God,
Lift smiling eyes through falling tears,
And, simply trusting, kiss the rod.

A NEW YEAR'S MENU

PUBLISHED IN THE *NATIONAL PROVISIONER*
JANUARY 8, 1916

Conscience, Clear

Kindness   Grace   Good Cheer

Tender Memories

Charity, Served with Discretion

Peace   Love   Truth

Long Life, Stuffed with Usefulness

Heart Fond and True
(A Large Portion)

Affection   Happiness

Best Wishes for Absent Friends

Mizpah

NEBRASKA PIONEERS

1917

Tune: "Tenting"

We are thinking tonight
   Of the old home farm
And the parents grown old and gray,
   The meadow, the brook
And the old farm house,
   And friends of an earlier day.
Many are the years
   Since those hardy Pioneers
Conquered this glorious West;
   Many noble States
Were settled, one by one,—
   Nebraska was the best.

CHORUS:
We are living tonight
   In comfort and peace,
Sheltered and safe from harm;
   Let's not forget
The old Pioneers
   On Nebraska's prairie farms.

In health and in sickness,
   In joy and in pain,
They opened this great virgin soil.
   They builded for better
Than ever they knew
   And we reaped the fruits of their toil.
All honor to them—
   The old Pioneers;
Their deeds to your children relate.
   In honoring them
We honor ourselves
   And doubly honor our State.

(Chorus)

THE HOME FLAG

AUGUST 1917

PUBLISHED IN THE *NATIONAL PROVISIONER*
SEPTEMBER 1, 1917

Each bright Star that shines
  In the Blue of Old Glory
    Twinkles for Home, Sweet Home.
The sweetest refrain
  Of its wonderful story
    Sing us of Home, Sweet Home.

The Red in its bars
Is the blood of our Fathers,
  Shed for our Home, Sweet Home.
Its pure virgin White
The sweet Mothers and Sisters,
    Queens in our Home, Sweet Home.

The Red, White and Blue
And the Stars of Old Glory,
  Fighting for Home, Sweet Home;
Bring Peace and Good Will
To Earth's war weary nations,
  Safety for Home, Sweet Home.

For Peace upon Earth
And Good Will among mortals,
  Happiness, Home, Sweet Home.
Oh, long may it wave,
This proud flag of our nation,
  Guarding our Home, Sweet Home.

AMERICAN BOYS

NOVEMBER 1917

PUBLISHED IN THE *NATIONAL PROVISIONER*
DECEMBER 1, 1917

American Boys:
   The best in all creation.
American Boys:
   The hope of ev'ry nation;
   Sons of sires that never quailed.
   Now when Liberty's assailed
   They are eager for the fight—
   Strong to battle for the right—
   For Columbia take their chance
   On the battle fields of France;
   With their Allies stand or fall,
   And for freedom stake their all.
   Shall we then our riches store
   While they face the battle's roar?
   Hoard our wheat and corn and cattle
   While they hear machineguns rattle?
   God pity him who in this strife
   Reckons gold above a life,
   In agony let him atone—
   Live to himself and die alone.

American Boys:
   On land or sea—
God bless all and keep them
   Wherever they may be.

NEBRASKA

PUBLISHED IN THE *NEBRASKA CITY NEWS*
JANUARY 18, 1918

From Plymouth Rock to Golden Gate,
    From Mobile to Alaska,
Columbia's priceless gems are set;
    Her em'rald is Nebraska.

The green of her alfalfa fields
    Shades to the waving corn,
And native grasses, rich and sweet,
    Her bosom fair adorn.

Where once the Ponca and Pawnee,
    The Otoe and the Sioux,
Chased buffalo o'er trackless wilds,
    Her thriving cities grew.

By silo, village, church and school
    The train and auto roam;
A proud, contented people sing,
    "Hail, Our Nebraska Home!"

Our fathers, hardy pioneers,
    In houses built of sod,
Laid the foundation, broad and deep,
    For freedom, home and God.

Let happy hearts in happy homes
    Still sing Nebraska's fame,
And may no selfishness or hate
    Cast shadow on her name.

TO ONE IN FRANCE

JUNE 1918

The rose buds in my garden,
    Sweet in the morning dew,
All glorious in the June time,
    Are singing to me of you.

"Over There" may the roses,
    Sweet in the morning dew,
'Mid all the death and terror,
    Tell sweetly my love to you.

BLACK JACK'S BOYS

PUBLISHED IN *THE RECRUIT: A NAVAL PICTORIAL MAGAZINE*
DECEMBER 1918

Tune: "Tramp, Tramp, Tramp"

1.
In the trenches here I sit,
Thinking, Mother, dear, of you.
And the dear old land of Freedom
    'cross the seas.
Waiting for the shells to drop;
Then, Hurrah! we're over the top,
And we'll bring our old friend Fritzie
    to his knees.

Chorus:
Boom! Boom! Boom!
The shells are falling—
How the bayonets do shine.
You can bet it takes some sand,
Charging over No Man's Land.
We've got to chase the Kaiser
    over the Rhine.

2.
Yankee Boys will not forget
All we owe to LaFayette,
And in Freedom's name we come to
    pay our score.
France and Belgium shall be free;
All the world have liberty;
All the oceans will be safe from shore
    to shore.

3.
When the battle's rage is done—
May all flags beneath the sun
Over free and happy nations peaceful
    wave;
And our Starry Banner free,
Bring the whole world liberty—
Man shall never more his fellow man
    enslave.

THE GOLDEN ROD HIGHWAY

AUGUST 26, 1919

Tune: "Long Trail"

Smiling all along the Highway,
    Waves the Golden Rod,
Giving promise of the richness
    Underneath the Sod.
Through the I-o-wa and Ne-bras-ka
    Leads the G. and R.
Guiding safely to their Journey's end,
    Happy Trav'lers from afar.

Chorus

There's a long, long trail a-winding
    From the East into the West,
Through a land of Milk and Honey,
    And this road's the best.
Come and travel o'er this Highway—
    It's the only thing to do—
Where the Golden Rod is glowing—
    There a welcome waits for you.

KENYON BILL

PUBLISHED IN THE *NATIONAL PROVISIONER*
SEPTEMBER 20, 1919

Kenyon Bill, Kenyon Bill,
   You have sure got lots to do;
Lay down your cards and show your hand,
   The packers are "calling" you!

PROGRESS

CHATHAM, ONTARIO
CIRCA 1922

If all progress you would block,
Get your hammer out and knock.
When anything comes up
That's for the town,
Take your stand out on the walk;
Never think—just talk and talk—
That's the way to put the Kibbosh
On the town.

If you want your town to grow,
Let the factories all know,
That everything home made
You mean to buy,—
Make them feel it is no bluff
That you sure will buy their stuff.
That's the way to put old town
Up Ace high.

A BIRTHDAY WISH

MAY 23, 1922

I hope that the sun may be shining,
But, even though skies be gray,
May your heart be full of sunshine
On this twenty-third of May.
This song, dear, my heart will be singing
When all other songs are sung:
"To me you're as fair as you were, dear,
When you and when I were young."

The years have travelled on swiftly
Since first you became my gal,
But, if they brought joy or sorrow,
They found you my staunch, good pal.
What the future may bring us
We know not—
But this is my wish, dear, today:
God give you sweet peace, love and gladness,
On each twenty-third day of May.

PROVISION—PROFIT—PROSPECT
(With Apologies to John W. Hall* for Infringing on His Doggerel Patent.)

PUBLISHED IN THE *NATIONAL PROVISIONER*
MAY 23, 1925

Price of hogs a-soaring.
Packers also "soreing,"
All the "Brains" a-snoring—
Makes one want to fight.
Salesmen all a-telling
How cheap John Jones is selling—
    However:
"No bird ever flies so high
But what he's got to light—
Gee, wot a life!"

---

* John W. Hall was one of C.M.'s colleagues in the meatpacking trade. One of his own bits of "doggerel" had presumably appeared in a recent *Provisioner* issue.

NEBRASKA

PUBLISHED IN THE *NEBRASKA STATE JOURNAL*

PUBLISHED IN THE *SUPERIOR EXPRESS*
JANUARY 27, 1927

The glories of Nebraska, let's sing both far and wide,
    That coming generations may in her gates abide.
Here health and wealth and plenty and peace and comfort dwell;
    The half of all her glory the tongue can never tell.

The mighty old Missouri her eastern borders sweep,
    The Platte and Niobrara her soils in moisture keep,
Her fruits and grain and grasses in rich abundance grow,
    And nature smiles so sweetly—no want our people know.

Here labor, farm and foundry work to the common good,
    And build up thriving cities where once the wigwam stood.
A sober, loyal people, with industry and thrift,
    Contented dwell in peaceful homes—the state's most precious gift.

As native sons and daughters of this our great home state,
    It is a sacred duty, we strive to keep it great.
The beauty spots God gave us, by us must not be shorn,
    But held in trust forever for children yet unborn.

MORAL
("With apologies to Brother Bill.")

PUBLISHED IN THE *NEBRASKA DAILY NEWS-PRESS*
JULY 23, 1927

For forty years we have been makin'
   Nebraska pigs into ham and bacon.
And if you want the best ham-and,
   Be sure you get the COUPON BRAND.
Nebraska City does her part,
   Right out here in the corn-belt heart,
And when you want your hams with eggs on—
   Be sure it's cured by—MORTON-GREGSON.

---

* This poem was evidently intended to be a play on Will M. Maupin's "Hymn to the Hog."

P.E.O. AND B.I.L.

"DEDICATED TO NEBRASKA CITY CHAPTER P.E.O."

NOVEMBER 17, 1927

These mystic letters give us thrill—
   Thrill more subdued and still
Less passionate but not less keen
   Than that which led our early youth
To consecrate our lives to truth.
   To search her out through all our days
And not forsake her simple ways.
   With steady faith in God above,
Our parents' God whose name is Love,
   Give justice to our fellow man
And act our part as best we can.
   Let Purity in thought and deed
Our daily life and actions lead.
   Oh! Happy youth and high ideals—
They thrill again. Our bosom feels
   As through our troubled years we go
Whene'er we see this P.E.O.

   Faith, Love, Purity, Justice, Truth—
The five-point Star we chose in youth
   To guide our ways we may have lost:
In crooked ways at frightful cost,
   Lost faith in virtue and in love,
Lost faith in justice, faith in truth.
   But feel again the thrill of youth.
Lift up your eyes and see the truth.
   The Star still shines that all may know
The Beauties of the P.E.O.

STAND UP FOR OTOE COUNTY

CIRCA 1928

Clear skies of blue and moonlight fair,
    With gentle breeze, pure glorious air;
Broad fields of grain and waving corn,
    With Redbirds whistling to the morn.
River and hills and stately trees,
    Red apples nodding in the breeze—
All are a part of God's great bounty
    That we enjoy in Otoe County.

MY VALENTINE

FEBRUARY 13, 1931

When life was young, my Valentine
Had hair of gold and lips of wine.
The lips are just as sweet today,
The gold is wondrous silver gray,
The years have made her still more fine,
And still she is my Valentine.

ROSES OF YOU

MARCH 13, 1934

The Rose Buds in my garden
Sweet with the morning dew,
All glorious in the June time,
Are singing to me of you.

Gone are the summer roses.
First is the morning dew,
But my heart, as in the June time,
Is singing to me of you.

God will protect his Roses.
When winter's cold is through,
In June He will send His Roses,
All singing to me of you.

APPENDIX

THE NORTHERN LAKES ARE CALLING

BY E.B. HAUSE

The Northern Lakes are calling:
Their voices bid me come:
I hear among the birches
The partridge roll his drum.

I have sorted o'er my tackle,
Tinkered reels & lines & hooks:
Oh. I'm tired of men and women,
Tired of work & noise & books.

I am tired of social functions,
Stiff, starched things & parted hair.
Want to loaf beside the campfire,
Wear a flannel shirt & swear:

Here's to Ho. SIR MILTON.

DEAR MILTON

BY E.B. HAUSE

ST. PAUL, MINNESOTA
FEBRUARY 16, 1922

An elixir of love to mine old head.
To drink the words your pen impart.
That genial smile and shimmering dome
Would mark you well, at the heavenly throne.
With lingering gaze we've studied your face
For lines that Time alone can trace,
Without a scuse of change or age
My! But you're smooth at camouflage.
We're pleased to note the ravage of years
Hasn't lessened the gray behind your ears.
If only that smile would broaden a bit
To offer a glimpse just under the lip,
We'd rest assured, the image is true
Of the friend we still have, the man we once knew.*

_____

* At the end of this poem-letter, "Doc" Hause wrote, "Thanks for the Photo."

NOTES

Acknowledgements

1. "City Packing House Exchange Burned," *Syracuse Journal Democrat*, January 19, 1934.

Introduction

2. "Elks' Memorial," *Nebraska City News*, December 9, 1913.
3. Ibid.
4. Ibid.

Chapter 1

5. "Carl M. Aldrich Can Remember the Indian: Manager of Morton-Gregson Was Born in Otoe County," *Nebraska Daily News-Press*, November 14, 1929.
6. The entry for Carl M. Aldrich in Watkins's *History of Nebraska* indicates that John and Mary Jane came to the Nebraska Territory in 1857. This is incorrect. According to Mary Jane's letters dated 1857, they had already been resident in Nebraska for at least one year.
7. Aldrich family genealogical records, Carl Milton Aldrich Collection.

8. John Aldrich, ed., *The Gleaner*, no. 3, February 1, year unknown, handwritten copy, John and Mary Jane Aldrich Collection.
9. "Carl M. Aldrich Can Remember the Indian."
10. Mary Jane Aldrich to her father, letter, December 17, 1857, John and Mary Jane Aldrich Collection.
11. The Aldriches' line of descent from William Brewster is recorded in Smith's *Jesse Smith*.
12. Baldwin and Baldwin, *Nebraskana*, 17.
13. Various sources document the lines of descent of William Howard Taft, Thomas Bailey Aldrich, Nelson W. Aldrich and Charles Sweetzer Aldrich from George Aldrich of Rhode Island.
14. Watkins, *History of Nebraska*, 489.
15. Crandall, *Obituary Notice of Dr. Laurens Hull*, 5.
16. Ibid., 4.
17. Watkins, *History of Nebraska*, 489.
18. Ibid.
19. Rogers, *Sidney Centennial Jubilee*, 27.
20. Ibid., 23.
21. Ibid., 28.
22. Ibid., 33.
23. Ibid.
24. Ibid., 33–35.
25. *History of Delaware County*, 284.
26. Mary Jane Aldrich to her father, letter, February 21, 1858, John and Mary Jane Aldrich Collection.
27. Ibid.
28. Turner, *In Memoriam*, 8.
29. Mary Jane Aldrich to her sister Dora, letter, November 9, 1857, John and Mary Jane Aldrich Collection.
30. Turner, *In Memoriam*, 8.
31. Watkins, *History of Nebraska*, 489.
32. *History of the State of Nebraska*, 1199. Settlement of the area had commenced a decade earlier. In 1846, the United States Army had established a military post, Fort Kearney, near present-day Nebraska City. The fort, however, had been abandoned by the time of the city's incorporation in 1855.
33. Ibid., 1204–5. Probably due to their comparatively brief sojourn in Nebraska and their even more abbreviated careers as local teachers, neither John's nor Mary Jane's name appears in any known annals of the history of Nebraska City education.

34. Mary Jane Aldrich, letter, date unknown, John and Mary Jane Aldrich Collection.
35. Turner, *In Memoriam*, 8.
36. Aldrich family genealogical records.
37. Mary Jane Aldrich to "My Own dear precious Mother," letter, October 25, 1857, John and Mary Jane Aldrich Collection.
38. Ibid.
39. "Carl M. Aldrich Can Remember the Indian."
40. Mary Jane Aldrich to "My Own dear precious Mother."
41. Ibid.
42. Ibid.
43. Ibid.
44. *History of the State of Nebraska*, 1193.
45. Mary Jane Aldrich to her father, letter, December 17, 1857.
46. Ibid.
47. Ibid.
48. Ibid.
49. Ibid.
50. Ibid.
51. Ibid.
52. Dale, *Otoe County Pioneers*, 32.
53. Watkins, *History of Nebraska*, 489.
54. "C.M. Aldrich Dies Suddenly Early Monday," *Nebraska Daily News-Press*, April 14, 1936.
55. *History of the State of Nebraska*, 1193.
56. Ibid., 1193–94.
57. Aldrich family genealogical records.
58. Ibid.
59. Ibid.
60. *History of the State of Nebraska*, 1200. Some of these slaves belonged to prominent citizen and future Wyoming congressman Stephen Nuckolls.
61. Ibid.
62. Ibid., 1194.
63. Ibid.
64. Turner, *In Memoriam*, 8.
65. *History of the State of Nebraska*, 1195.
66. Ibid.
67. Ibid.

68. Dale, *Otoe County Pioneers*, 32. Otoe County's sparse population also meant that John was required to take an active role in civic affairs. He was called for jury duty at least twice in 1860.
69. Ibid.
70. "Witter H. Johnston" in *Annals of Iowa* 10 (1911), 156.
71. Ibid.
72. Martin, *General Henry Baxter*, 6.
73. Ibid.
74. Ibid., 16–32.
75. Henry Baxter subsequently served as minister to Honduras for President Ulysses S. Grant. A full account of General Baxter's life is found in Martin's book *General Henry Baxter*.
76. "Carl M. Aldrich Can Remember the Indian."
77. Dale, *Otoe County Pioneers*, 32.
78. "Carl M. Aldrich Can Remember the Indian."
79. Mary Jane Aldrich, letter, date unknown.
80. Ibid.
81. "Carl M. Aldrich Can Remember the Indian."
82. Ibid.

Chapter 2

83. "A Pioneer Song," *Nebraska Daily News-Press*, November 19, 1929.
84. Ibid.
85. Turner, *In Memoriam*, 9.
86. Ibid.
87. *History of Delaware County*, 284.
88. The reverend's sons Witter and Hughy bought out their sisters and became sole proprietors of the family homestead. *History of Delaware County*, 284.
89. Walker, *Pioneer Collections*, 247.
90. 1910 and 1920 United States Federal Censuses.
91. Willard and Livermore, *Woman of the Century*, 17.
92. Turner, *In Memoriam*, 9.
93. Mary Jane Aldrich to her brother Witter, letter, July 19, 1867, John and Mary Jane Aldrich Collection.
94. Cedar Rapids 1869 City Directory.
95. Turner, *In Memoriam*, 9.

96. Mary Jane Aldrich to her brother Witter.

97. Scrapbook of Mary Jane Aldrich, John and Mary Jane Aldrich Collection.

98. Carl Milton Aldrich, essay "House," date unknown, Carl Milton Aldrich Collection.

99. Baldwin and Baldwin, *Nebraskana*, 17.

100. Carl Milton Aldrich, essay "Sun," date unknown, Carl Milton Aldrich Collection.

101. Baldwin and Baldwin, *Nebraskana*, 17.

102. "Countrywide News Notes," *National Provisioner*, August 31, 1935.

103. Woodhead, *Shopping, Seduction & Mr. Selfridge*, 9.

104. Ibid., 6. Like her cousin Mary Jane, Lois was religious and (according to Selfridge biographer Lindy Woodhead) "abhorred alcohol."

105. Ibid., 5–7. Harry and Carl had much in common. A few years older than Carl, Harry began his career in the retail business much as his second cousin did—as a lowly stock boy in Field's wholesale department. Like Carl would, he gained practical experience as a traveling salesman and subsequently made ample use of his inborn resourcefulness, initiative and strong work ethic to become one of the world's most legendary retail magnates. Even Harry and Carl's personal lives mirrored each other's to a remarkable extent. Both were devoted to their mothers. Both, as young boys, devoured the spellbinding frontier stories of James Fenimore Cooper—stories reminiscent of the backwoods exploits of their great-grandfather Colonel Witter Johnston. Although short men, both were considered physically attractive and possessed undeniable charisma. Both would marry into affluent Illinois families and raise five children. (Carl and his wife would adopt their oldest grandchild.) In one significant aspect, Harry and Carl's fortunes differed. Carl would never attain the same dizzy heights of fame and fortune that Harry did. He would, however, die solvent, whereas Harry ended his days destitute.

106. Cedar Rapids 1869 City Directory.

107. 1870 United States Federal Census.

108. Aldrich family genealogical records. Carl's reputation in the meatpacking industry possibly helped pave the way for John Jr., who worked at one point for the Swift & Company, one of Carl's own employers.

109. "Sixty Years on the Job," *National Provisioner*, April 18, 1936.

110. Mary Jane Aldrich, "A Tribute from a Mother to her Son," Carl Milton Aldrich Collection.

111. Turner, *In Memoriam*, 11. Carl continued to provide for both his parents and his unmarried sister up to their deaths in old age.

112. Warren, *Tied to the Great Packing Machine*, 31.
113. Ibid.
114. Ibid.
115. Hudson, Bergman and Horton, *Biographical Dictionary of Iowa*, 469.
116. Rasdal, *Czech Village & New Bohemia*, 26. Cedar Rapids benefited from its proximity to the Cedar River. However, when Thomas McElderry Sinclair first arrived in town, there was no railroad. According to an entry for Sinclair found at the website Coe College: The First Hundred Years, he "worked fourteen-hour days in order to build up everything needed for his community."
117. Hudson, Bergman and Horton, *Biographical Dictionary of Iowa*, 469.
118. Ibid.
119. Ibid.
120. Peel-Austin to Brupbacher, email. One of Sinclair's daughters followed in his footsteps by serving as a missionary to China, where she was later killed in the Boxer Rebellion.
121. Barr, *History of T.M. Sinclair & Company*, 8.
122. Blumenthal, *Bootleg*, 17.
123. Ibid.
124. Ibid., 20.
125. Ibid., 23.
126. Ibid., 25–26.
127. Ibid., 26.
128. Ibid.
129. Ibid., 25–27.
130. Willard and Livermore, *Woman of the Century*, 17.
131. Ibid.
132. Ibid.
133. Ibid.
134. Handwritten temperance pledge, 1875, Carl Milton Aldrich Collection.
135. T.M. Sinclair Co., "To Whom It May Concern," letter, February 1, 1884, Carl Milton Aldrich Collection.
136. James Macauley, letter, February 1884, Carl Milton Aldrich Collection.
137. James Macauley, letter, December 31, 1898, Carl Milton Aldrich Collection.
138. Milton Johnston to his grandson, letter, February 1, 1882, Carl Milton Aldrich Collection.
139. *National Cyclopedia of American Biography*, 475.
140. Ibid. Weare's best-remembered venture came several years after Carl worked for him. In the early 1890s, he arranged for the construction of

a five-hundred-ton river steamer named after him. This boat "was built and launched in time to take a cargo from an ocean steamer and ascend the Yukon to the Klondike that fall, with the result that rich and extensive placer gold mines, as well as quartz, coal, copper and other materials, were opened up to the world."

141. Another protégé of Weare's was outlaw-turned-lawman Josiah Horner, also known as Frank M. Canton. Weare would give the job of superintendent of the Nebraska City Packing Company to Canton in the early 1890s. Canton's story can be read in DeArment's *Alias Frank Canton*.

142. "It Was Some Time Ago," *Nebraska City Weekly News*, March 28, 1924. A December 1882 write-up in the *Nebraska City News* indicates that J. Sterling Morton delivered an address on the grand opening of the Nebraska & Iowa packinghouse in late 1882.

143. *History of the State of Nebraska*, 1215.

144. Jim McKee, "Packing, Canning Once Big Business in Nebraska City," *Lincoln Journal Star*, December 14, 2019.

145. *History of the State of Nebraska*, 1215.

146. Calhoun, *Nebraska City*, 5.

147. According to the *History of the State of Nebraska*, Lloyd was also apparently treasurer of the Nebraska & Iowa Packing Company as of 1882.

148. "It Was Some Time Ago."

149. Ibid.

150. Ibid.

151. Olson, *J. Sterling Morton*, 35.

152. Ibid., 50.

153. "Carl Aldrich Can Remember the Indian."

154. Olson, *J. Sterling Morton*, 50.

155. Ibid., 77.

156. Ibid., 79.

157. Ibid., 156–57.

158. Ibid., 161.

159. Ibid., 163–65.

160. Ibid., 166.

161. Nebraska City was also recovering from a major flood that had struck the region two years earlier. *History of the State of Nebraska*, 1194.

162. Ibid., 1199.

163. "It Was Some Time Ago."

164. Ibid.

165. Ibid.

Chapter 3

166. Ibid.

167. Ibid.

168. Ibid.

169. "Carl M. Aldrich Can Remember the Indian."

170. "Hotel Arrivals," *Daily American*, May 17, 1885.

171. "Social and Personal," *Record-Union*, February 1, 1886.

172. *Combined History of Shelby and Moultrie Counties*, 44.

173. Ibid., 153.

174. Homer H. Cooper, "The Lincoln-Thornton Debate: 1856, Shelbyville, Illinois," in *Journal of the Illinois State Historical Society* 10, no. 1 (April 1917): 113.

175. Fraker, *Lincoln's Ladder to the Presidency*, 123.

176. Cooper, *Journal of the Illinois State Historical Society*, 121.

177. Ibid., 103.

178. Ibid., 111.

179. "Doctor John Durkee," *Durkee Family Newsletter*, Winter 1985.

180. *Portrait and Biographical Record*, 454.

181. Reser, *Grist Mills of Tippecanoe County*, 68–74. It was near Durkee's Grist Mill that it was believed the notorious Reno gang stashed $96,000 worth of ill-gotten (and never recovered) gold years later.

182. Cooper, *Journal of the Illinois State Historical Society*, 113.

183. Ibid., 118.

184. "William J. Tackett: Was a '49er' and Afterwards Practiced Medicine Here," unknown newspaper, unknown date (presumably 1905).

185. Ibid.

186. Ibid.

187. *Portrait and Biographical Record*, 454.

188. Ibid.

189. Aldrich family genealogical records.

190. *Essays by May Tackett*, 1884, Carl Milton Aldrich Collection.

191. *The Review*, December 23, 1885.

192. "Married," publisher unknown, date unknown.

193. Aldrich family genealogical records.

194. C.M. Aldrich, "Stockyards, Packing and Provision Houses," in *Brief History of Peoria*, 33–34.

195. Bordin, *Frances Willard*, 79.

196. Ibid., 108.

197. Ibid., 106.

198. Ibid., 68–69.

199. Ibid., 129–30.

200. Foster, *Truth in the Case*, 18.

201. Ibid., 21.

202. Ibid., 11.

203. Ibid., 21.

204. Ibid.

205. Ibid., 19–20.

206. "National Crusaders," *Courier-Journal*, January 24, 1890.

207. Foster, *Truth in the Case*, 12.

208. "History," Travelers Protective Association.

209. "Current Events," *Logansport Daily Reporter*, April 11, 1892.

210. "Travelers' Association Elects Officers."

211. "Commercial Travelers at the Fair," *Chicago Tribune*, June 8, 1893. Mary Jane Aldrich also spoke at the 1893 World's Fair. She delivered an address titled "Woman as a Law Giver."

212. "The Traveling Men," *St. Louis Daily Globe*, June 8, 1893.

213. "The Traveling Men," *St. Louis Daily Globe*, June 9, 1893.

214. "The Traveling Men," *St. Joseph Herald*, February 6, 1895.

215. "T.P.A. Notes," *Logansport Pharos-Tribune*, July 16, 1893.

216. "Asking Aid from Congress," *Memphis Commercial*, September 29, 1893.

217. "To Prohibit Ticket Scalping," *Washington Times*, April 7, 1894.

218. "Traveling Men Form a Club," *Daily Inter Ocean*, March 26, 1894.

219. "Policy Not Changed," *Daily Inter Ocean*, June 23, 1894.

220. "TPA," *Fort Wayne Daily Gazette*, September 30, 1894.

221. "TPA," *Fort Wayne Daily Gazette*, October 21, 1894.

222. Ibid.

223. "Commercial Men's Bill Passed," *Daily Inter Ocean*, February 14, 1895.

224. The United States House of Representatives itself apparently saw no real need for the passage of such legislation. On January 9, 1895, the *Chicago Tribune* reported:

> *The House committee on Inter-State Commerce reported back…that in their opinion there was nothing in the inter-State commerce law to prevent the railroads issuing such tickets, and the only object of the present bill was declaratory, so that the commercial men could be accommodated by the railroads without any possibility of infringing the law. The committee, however, amended the original bill so as to require railroads which issue these joint tickets to file with the Inter-State Commerce Commission copies*

*of the joint tariffs of rates, and further placing these tickets and tariffs
under the control of the commission.*

225. "Opposed to the 5,000-Mile Tickets," *Chicago Tribune*, February 15, 1895.

226. "Defends the New Mileage Book," *Pittsburgh Post*, January 26, 1897.

227. Ibid.

228. Crandall, *Obituary Notice of Dr. Laurens Hull*, 5.

229. Aldrich family genealogical records.

230. Nash, Jeffrey, Howe, Frederick, Davis and Winkler, *American People*, 663–64.

231. Ibid., 664–67, 670–71.

232. Ibid., 667.

233. "National Director Aldrich Here," *St. Louis Post-Dispatch*, May 13, 1895.

234. "C.M. Aldrich Dies Suddenly."

235. Dunlap, *Charles Gates Dawes*, 39.

236. Ibid., 37.

237. Ibid., 23–24.

238. C.M. and Dawes apparently renewed their acquaintance years later when, in late 1922, C.M.'s son Glen became a speaker for the Smyrna Special Relief Committee. Dawes, lately the first director of the Bureau of the Budget, served as treasurer of the Committee.

239. Dunlap, *Charles Gates Dawes*, 33.

240. Ibid., 15.

241. Nash, Jeffrey, Howe, Frederick, Davis and Winkler, *American People*, 671.

242. Bryan's defeat did not discourage him from pursuing a political career. Today best known for his role in the Scopes Trial of 1925, he ran for president of the United States twice more and served as secretary of state in Woodrow Wilson's administration.

243. Dunlap, *Charles Gates Dawes*, 49–51.

244. Ibid., 198–99.

245. Ibid., 220.

246. Ibid., 178–79.

247. "Want Government Jobs," *Fort Wayne Daily Gazette*, April 18, 1897.

248. *Fort Wayne Daily Gazette*, September 26, 1897.

249. "TPA," *Fort Wayne Sunday Gazette*, September 26, 1897.

Chapter 4

250. "Articles Are Filed," *Gazette*, March 9, 1899.

251. Charles B. Soutter to "My dear Carl," letter, December 23, 1898, Carl Milton Aldrich Collection.

252. *Cedar Rapids Evening Gazette*, December 27, 1898.

253. Warren, *Tied to the Great Packing Machine*, 31.

254. Turner, *In Memoriam*, 13.

255. "Packing Company Reorganizes," *Fremont Tri-Weekly Tribune*, March 11, 1899.

256. Charles B. Soutter to "My dear Carl."

257. *Cedar Rapids Evening Gazette*, December 27, 1898.

258. Warren, *Tied to the Great Packing Machine*, 15–16.

259. Warren, *Tied to the Great Packing Machine*, 31.

260. Louis F. Swift to C.M. Aldrich, letter, December 5, 1899, Carl Milton Aldrich Collection.

261. *All Roads Lead to Citronelle*, Citronelle Historical Preservation Society.

262. Ibid.

263. "Enormous Increase in Sales," *Chicago Tribune*, January 6, 1899.

264. Louis F. Swift to C.M. Aldrich, letter, December 5, 1899, Carl Milton Aldrich Collection. C.M. scribbled on the back to his wife, "May, Keep this letter for me—CMA."

265. H.C.S. to C.M. Aldrich, letter, December 21, 1899, Carl Milton Aldrich Collection.

266. Various to C.M. Aldrich, letter December 23, 1899, Carl Milton Aldrich Collection.

267. L.F. Swift to C.M. Aldrich, letter, January 10, 1900, Carl Milton Aldrich Collection.

268. Warren, *Tied to the Great Packing Machine*, 33.

269. Ibid.

270. "Butchers Walk Out at South St. Paul," *Saint Paul Globe*, July 13, 1904.

271. "Thomas M. Sinclair," Coe College.

272. Barr, *History of T.M. Sinclair & Company*, 4.

273. L.F. Swift to C.M. Aldrich, May 17, 1905, Carl Milton Aldrich Collection.

274. "Swift & Co.," *Commercial and Financial Chronicle*, December 1, 1906.

275. "View of the Pork Packing Establishment of J.Y. Griffin & Co."

276. Ibid.

277. Ibid.

278. "Final Day for the Exhibition," *Winnipeg Tribune*, July 28, 1905.
279. Ibid.
280. "Manitoba Meat Trade," *Winnipeg Tribune*, February 22, 1906.
281. "Packing Business Sold," *Victoria Daily Times*, June 5, 1906.
282. Ibid.
283. "Swift & Co."
284. "C.M. Aldrich Dies Suddenly."
285. Ibid.
286. Ibid.
287. "Cattle Are Now Shipped Dressed," *Winnipeg Tribune*, September 29, 1906.
288. Ibid.
289. "Swift & Co."
290. Ibid.

Chapter 5

291. "The Jack Pot," *St. Joseph News-Press*, March 25, 1907.
292. Calhoun, *Nebraska City*, 5. Portus B. Weare and other members of the Weare family were listed as directors of the Nebraska City Packing Company in the 1902 volume of *Directory of Directors in the City of Chicago*.
293. Calhoun, *Nebraska City*, 5–6.
294. J. Sterling Morton donated considerable acreage and assisted in raising funds for this second packing plant. John W. Steinhart, "Plant Trees," *Nebraska Horticulture* 10, no. 4 (April 1921).
295. Ibid.
296. "William Linaker Gregson," *Successful American*, March 1902.
297. McKee, "Packing, Canning Once Big Business."
298. Various publications provide contradictory information about Nebraska City's early packing companies and the series of subsequent takeovers. According to John W. Steinhart's "Plant Trees," the Chicago Packing and Provision Company had taken over both packing plants and "operated them for a long period" before J. Sterling Morton persuaded his sons to purchase them.
299. Taylor, *History of the Board of Trade of the City of Chicago*, 136.
300. "William Linaker Gregson."

301. Leidigh and Cooper, *Nebraska City*, 8.
302. United States Federal Trade Commission, *Report of the Federal Trade Commission on the Meat-Packing Industry*, 146–47. Labor strife also evidently thwarted the company's early operations.
303. "Chicago Section," *National Provisioner*, December 21, 1907.
304. "Change at Packing House," *Nebraska City News*, July 23, 1907.
305. "Will Probably Start," *Nebraska City News*, February 5, 1901.
306. "Personal Equation Important," *National Provisioner*, October 24, 1925.
307. "Your Price Is Your Pride," *National Provisioner*, April 16, 1924.
308. "Here's a 'Sell-Right' Story," *National Provisioner*, October 2, 1926.
309. "The Passing Show," *Nebraska Press*, November 8 (year unknown).
310. "Profit in Healthy Hogs."
311. Warren, *Tied to the Great Packing Machine*, 145.
312. "Care and Cleanliness in Meat Packing," *National Provisioner*, June 18, 1910.
313. Ibid.
314. Ibid.
315. Ibid.
316. Ibid.
317. Ibid.
318. Ibid.
319. Ibid.
320. Ballowe, *Man of Salt and Trees*, 170.
321. "New Nebraska Packing Concern," *National Provisioner*, November 16, 1912. C.M.'s partners in this enterprise were George M. Thomas, Richard Laidlaw, Walter Y. Dowe and William Kennedy.
322. "New Nebraska Packing Concern."
323. Federal Trade Commission, *Report of the Federal Trade Commission on the Meat-Packing Industry*, 146–47.
324. "Chicago Section," *National Provisioner*, December 30, 1922.
325. Scrapbook of Carl Milton Aldrich, Carl Milton Aldrich Collection.

Chapter 6

326. "The Flowers That Bloom, Tra-La!" *Nebraska Daily News-Press*, March 17, 1927.

327. "He Reports Seeing Year's First Robin," *Nebraska Daily News-Press*, January 22, 1928.

328. "Aldrich Says Poison Kills," *Nebraska Daily News-Press*, May 7, 1926.

329. "Purchased a Home," *Nebraska City News*, June 15, 1909.

330. Scrapbook of Carl Milton Aldrich.

331. "Will Miss His Flowers," unknown newspaper, unknown date (circa 1922).

332. Ibid.

333. "Beautifying City Garden Club Topic," *Nebraska Daily News-Press*, April 2, 1936.

334. "The Kick Kolumn," *Nebraska Daily News-Press*, April 4, 1928.

335. "'C.M.' Raises Flowers and 'C.P.' Pigeons," *Nebraska Daily News-Press*, June 10, 1930.

336. "Willfully Destroy Property," *Nebraska City News*, September 21, 1915.

337. "May Go Slow," *Nebraska City News*, May 14, 1915.

338. "Carves Some Judgments," *Nebraska City News*, May 8, 1917.

339. "Beautifying City Garden Club Topic."

340. Olson, *J. Sterling Morton*, 163.

341. *Organization of the Nebraska State Board of Horticulture*, 22.

342. Olson, *J. Sterling Morton*, 163.

343. Ibid., 163–64.

344. "The City," *Nebraska State Journal*, January 5, 1872.

345. Olson, *J. Sterling Morton*, 165.

346. Ibid.

347. Ibid., 166.

348. "Arbor Day Proclamation," *Omaha Daily Bee*, April 17, 1885.

349. "Adopt Program for Arbor Day. Arrangement Committee Report on Celebration to Be Held Here April 23," unknown newspaper, unknown date.

350. "Planning Big Celebration," *Nebraska City News*, March 2, 1917.

351. "A City Flag," *Nebraska City News*, July 2, 1915.

352. Writing to their youngest son in 1932, May Aldrich expressed regret that business took her husband out of town that spring: "Dad was in Chicago all last week....I feel sorry to think he had to be away for the Arbor Day celebration, he had done so much to make it a success." May

Aldrich to Ralf Aldrich, letter, Wednesday the 27th, Ralf Johnston Aldrich Collection.

353. Newspaper unknown, date unknown. Found in the scrapbook of Carl Milton Aldrich.

354. "Elks' Memorial."

355. "1930 Arbor Day Observed Here," *Nebraska Daily News-Press*, April 23, 1930.

356. Ibid.

357. Egleston, *Arbor Day Leaves*, 1.

358. Ibid., 8.

359. Ibid., 9–10.

360. Ibid., 13.

361. Ibid., 20.

362. Ibid., 25.

363. Ibid., 27.

364. Ibid., 28.

365. "C.M.A.," *Nebraska Daily News-Press*, April 16, 1936.

366. "My Three Books," *Nebraska Daily News-Press*, January 22, 1927.

367. Ibid.

368. "Adventure Stories Were Favorites," *Nebraska Daily News-Press*, December 7, 1930.

369. "Mr. Howe's Novel," *Nebraska Daily News-Press*, April 10, 1930.

370. Personal library of C.M. Aldrich, Carl Milton Aldrich Collection.

371. "C.M. Aldrich Dies Suddenly."

372. Scrapbook of Carl Milton Aldrich.

Chapter 7

373. Ibid. Sweet, a Republican like C.M., later represented Nebraska's First District in the U.S. House of Representatives.

374. "C.M.A."

375. Ibid.

376. "The Kick Kolumn," *Nebraska Daily News-Press*, February 23, 1929.

377. "C.M.A."

378. "Personalities," *National Provisioner*, October 20, 1917.

379. "Personal and Otherwise," *National Provisioner*, October 17, 1908.

380. "Chicago Section," *National Provisioner*, May 13, 1911.

381. "Who's Who and Why," *National Provisioner*, October 24, 1914.

382. "Chicago Section," *National Provisioner*, January 7, 1911.

383. "Chicago Section," *National Provisioner*, March 18, 1911.

384. Turner, *In Memoriam*, 14.

385. John Aldrich Jr.'s wife, Ethel, was, like C.M., an avid gardener who cultivated prize-winning flowers.

386. John Aldrich to Carl Milton Aldrich, letter, October 4, 1909, Carl Milton Aldrich Collection.

387. Ibid.

388. Ibid.

389. "Local Brevities," *Nebraska City News*, December 31, 1909.

390. "C.M.A."

391. "A Bit of Pleasant Wayside Gossip," *Reading Times*, October 6, 1909.

392. "A Hymn to Efficiency," *Nebraska Daily News-Press*, May 28, 1930.

393. "C.M. Aldrich Dies Suddenly."

394. *Nebraska State Journal*, January 16, 1910.

395. "A Man of Action," *Nebraska Daily News-Press*, April 15, 1936.

396. "Waltonians Plan for Movie Program," *Nebraska Daily News-Press*, March 24, 1927.

397. "Frank Reavis to Speak on Tuesday," *Nebraska Daily News-Press*, February 11, 1928.

398. "Two Parties to Meet April 26," *Nebraska Daily News-Press*, April 12, 1928.

399. "C.M. Aldrich Dies Suddenly."

400. "Mrs. Blanchard President," *Lincoln Journal-Star*, January 13, 1925.

401. Ibid.

402. C.M. wrote the following letter to the editor, which appeared in the *Nebraska City News* on June 8, 1915:

> *Mayor Katzenstein's proposition for* [a] *swimming pool at Morton Park certainly should be carried through to a conclusion. Nothing could be of more benefit to us as a community or be of more help to the youth of our city as well as the older people.*
>
> *We should have a good, liberal sized concrete basin and provision made for moderate sized dressing rooms and a regular park policeman in charge. I feel sure that every one in the city would very gladly vote for a reasonable expenditure in that direction, and we will all be willing to help individually in a reasonable way if it is decided to raise any part of the funds by subscription.*
>
> *Don't let the idea get cold; let's put it through and have the benefit of it this summer.*

With a swimming pool of this kind at the park and decent toilet arrangements in the park, [I] believe that hundreds of families will come from out of town to camp at the park during the Chautauqua season at least. They do it at other places and will here if we provide the facilities.

Yours truly,
C.M. Aldrich.

403. "A Man of Action."
404. Ibid.
405. "How Times Flies! Forty-Five Years ago," *Nebraska City News-Press*, September 6, 1953.
406. "A Man of Action." C.M.'s "time in Canada" may allude either to his residence in Winnipeg during the early 1900s or to the year he spent away from Nebraska City (1922–23) managing Wilson & Co.'s packing plant in Chatham, Ontario.
407. Ibid.
408. Baldwin and Baldwin, *Nebraskana*, 17.
409. "24 More Names for Commercial Club Membership Roll," *Lincoln Daily Star*, April 19, 1917.
410. "C.M. Aldrich Dies Suddenly."
411. "Nebraska State Volunteer Fireman's Association," *Alliance Herald*, January 28, 1915.
412. "New Platform for Industry," *Beatrice Daily Sun*, December 7, 1928.
413. Certificate: Arthur J. Weaver's appointment of C.M. Aldrich as a delegate to the Mississippi Valley Convention at St. Louis, November 11 and 18, 1929, Carl Milton Aldrich Collection.
414. "C.M. Aldrich Dies Suddenly."
415. Baldwin and Baldwin, *Nebraskana*, 17.
416. "A Man of Action."
417. Baldwin and Baldwin, *Nebraskana*, 17.
418. "A Man of Action."
419. *In the World War*, 10.
420. "Off for France," *Nebraska City News*, June 26, 1917.
421. Ralf Johnston Aldrich, application for retirement, Ralf Johnston Aldrich Collection.
422. "They Are Separated Far from One Another," *Nebraska City News*, July 2, 1918.
423. "Each Did Their Bit," *Nebraska City News*, June 26, 1917.
424. "Ralf Over in France," *Nebraska City News*, October 2, 1917.

425. "May Go to Observers School," *Nebraska City News*, October 4, 1918.

426. "Meets Gen. Pershing," *Nebraska City News*, April 2, 1918.

427. "The Guns That Count," *Nebraska City News*, July 23, 1918.

428. "People You Know," *Lincoln Journal Star*, March 31, 1919.

429. "Observe Flag Day," *Nebraska City News*, June 19, 1917.

430. Ibid.

431. Ralf Johnston Aldrich, application.

432. Wikkerink to Brupbacher, email.

433. Ibid.

434. Greene, *Who's Who in Canada*, 1152.

435. "Centennial 1954," *Nebraska City News-Press*, October 21, 1953.

436. "Nebraska D.A.R. to Meet in June at Arbor Lodge," *Plattsmouth Journal*, May 14, 1928.

437. "Virginia Alice Cottey," Cottey College.

438. "Mrs. Carl Aldrich Dead," *Nebraska City News*, February 25, 1913.

439. "Faculty Names Honor Students," *Nebraska Daily News-Press*, April 2, 1927.

440. "In Memorium: Betty Mallery," obituary pamphlet, March 27, 2004, Carl Milton Aldrich Collection.

441. "Our Garden," unknown newspaper (Nebraska City), unknown date (circa 1920).

442. "Appoint Y.M.C.A. Committee," *Nebraska State Journal*, June 22, 1910.

443. "A Man of Action."

444. "Campfire Girls Win New Honors," *Nebraska Daily News-Press*, July 6, 1927.

445. A.H. DeLong, "Otoe County Farm Bureau Notes," *Nebraska Daily News-Press*, October 5, 1928.

446. "KK: An Appreciation," unknown newspaper, unknown date.

447. C.M. Aldrich, "Lincoln Day Speech," Carl Milton Aldrich Collection.

Chapter 8

448. "The Firemen's Banquet," *Nebraska City News*, April 9, 1915.

449. Ibid.

450. Ibid.

451. "The Advent of a New Community Institution," *Nebraska Daily News-Press*, February 13, 1927.

452. "Sales Head Honored," *National Provisioner*, November 30, 1929.

453. Ibid.

454. Ibid.

455. "Has Business Come Back?" *National Provisioner*, March 29, 1930.

456. Ibid.

457. Ibid.

458. "Packing Plant Is Valuable Asset," *Nebraska Daily News-Press*, March 13, 1932.

459. Ibid.

460. Ibid.

461. Ibid.

462. Ibid.

463. Ibid.

464. Partsch, *Nebraska City: Images of America*, 75.

465. "Late Mr. Aldrich Honored by Club," *Nebraska Daily News-Press*, May 7, 1936.

466. "Nebraska City Packing Plant Humming Again," *Nebraska Daily News-Press*, August 29, 1933.

467. "Government to Operate Local Packing House," *Nebraska Daily News-Press*, August 17, 1934.

468. Ibid.

469. "Plant Blaze Is Seen 40 Miles Away," *Nebraska Daily News-Press*, January 16, 1934.

470. "City Packing House Exchange Burned."

471. Ibid.

472. "New Nebraska Packing Concern."

473. "Countrywide News Notes."

474. "C.M. Aldrich Dies Suddenly."

475. Ibid.

476. "Flowers of Spring Behind Schedule," *Nebraska Daily News-Press*, March 29, 1936.

477. "C.M. Aldrich Dies Suddenly."

478. "Nebraska City Packing Plant Humming Again."

479. Scrapbook of Carl Milton Aldrich.

480. "Sixty Years on the Job."

481. "C.M. Aldrich Dies Suddenly."

482. "Final Rites Held for C.M. Aldrich," *Nebraska Daily News-Press*, April 17, 1936.

483. "Aldrich Record Is 100 Per Cent Upon All Lines," *Nebraska Daily News-Press*, April 14, 1936.

484. "Dr. Sisson to Be 80 on Saturday," *Nebraska Daily News-Press*, November 20, 1931.
485. Baldwin and Baldwin, *Nebraskana*, 1102.
486. Scrapbook of Carl Milton Aldrich.
487. "Nebraska City Observes 64th Arbor Day Fete," *Nebraska City Daily News-Press*, April 23, 1936.
488. Scrapbook of Carl Milton Aldrich.
489. "A Man of Action."

BIBLIOGRAPHY

Archival Sources

Carl Milton Aldrich Collection. Held by Rachel Brupbacher.
John and Mary Jane Aldrich Collection. Held by Rachel Brupbacher.
Ralf Johnston Aldrich Collection. Held privately.

Author Correspondence

Peel-Austin, Jessica, museum program manager at Brucemore, to Rachel Brupbacher. Email, September 10, 2021.
Wikkerink, Karen Aldrich, to Rachel Brupbacher. Email, May 24, 2020.

Books and Pamphlets

All Roads Lead to Citronelle. Citronelle Historical Preservation Society, April 2011.
Baldwin, Sara Mullin, and Robert Morton, eds. *Nebraskana: Biographical Sketches of Nebraska Men and Women of Achievement Who Have Been Awarded Life Membership in the Nebraskana Society.* Hebron, NE: Baldwin Company, 1932.
Ballowe, James. *A Man of Salt and Trees: The Life of Joy Morton.* Dekalb: Northern Illinois University Press, 2009.

Barr, Eric. *History of T.M. Sinclair & Company, Meatpacking Plant*. Hiawatha, IA: J&A Printing, n.d.

Blumenthal, Karen. *Bootleg: Murder, Moonshine, and the Lawless Years of Prohibition*. New York: Roaring Brook Press, 2011.

Bordin, Ruth. *Frances Willard: A Biography*. Chapel Hill: University of North Carolina Press, 1986.

A Brief History of Peoria. 1896.

Bulletin of Drury College 15, no. 3 (July 1915). Springfield, MO, Drury College.

Calhoun, S.J., Jr. *Nebraska City: A Reflex of Its Importance as a Commercial and Manufacturing Center*. Nebraska City, NE: Staats-Zeitung Printing House, 1888.

Combined History of Shelby and Moultrie Counties, Illinois: With Illustrations Descriptive of Their Scenery and Biographical Sketches of Some of Their Prominent Men and Pioneers. Philadelphia: Brink, McDonough & Co., 1881.

Crandall, C.M. *Obituary Notice of Dr. Laurens Hull*. Albany: Van Benthuysen & Sons' Steam Printing House, 1867.

Dale, Raymond E. *Otoe County Pioneers: A Biographical Dictionary*. Lincoln, NE, 1961.

DeArment, Robert K. *Alias Frank Canton*. Norman: University of Oklahoma Press, 1997.

Directory of Directors in the City of Chicago. 1902.

Dunlap, Annette B. *Charles Gates Dawes: A Life*. Evanston, IL: Northwestern University Press and the Evanston History Center, 2016.

Egleston, N.H. *Arbor Day Leaves*. New York: American Book Company, 1893.

Foster, J. Ellen. *The Truth in the Case: Concerning Partisanship and Non-partisanship in the W.C.T.U.* N.p., 1889.

Fraker, Guy C. *Lincoln's Ladder to the Presidency: The Eighth Judicial Circuit*. Carbondale: Southern Illinois University Press, 2012.

Greene, B.M. *Who's Who in Canada, 1927: An Illustrated Biographical Record of Men and Women of the Time*. Toronto: International Press Limited, 1927.

The History of Delaware County, N.Y. New York: W.W. Munsell & Co., 1880.

History of the State of Nebraska. Chicago: Western Historical Company, A.T. Andreas, Proprietor, 1882.

Hudson, David, Marvin Bergman and Loren Horton, eds. *The Biographical Dictionary of Iowa*. Iowa City: University of Iowa Press, 2008.

In the World War 1917–1918–1919 Otoe County Nebraska. W.K. Keithley, M.J. Wilkins, R.P. Laurance, C.E. Powlder, January 1, 1919.

Leidigh and Cooper. *Nebraska City: The Most Beautiful City of Nebraska as It Is Today in Story and Pictures*. Nebraska City, NE: Press of the Morton Printing Co., 1906.

Martin, Jay C. *General Henry Baxter, 7ᵗʰ Michigan Volunteer Infantry: A Biography*. Jefferson, NC: McFarland & Company, Inc. Publishers, 2016.

Nash, Gary B., Julie Roy Jeffrey, John R. Howe, Peter J. Frederick, Allen F. Davis and Allan M. Winkler, eds. *The American People: Creating a Nation and a Society*. Vol, 2, second ed. New York: HarperCollins, 1990.

The National Cyclopedia of American Biography. Vol. 10. New York: James T. White & Company, 1900.

Olson, James C. *J. Sterling Morton*. Lincoln: University of Nebraska Press, 1942.

Organization of the Nebraska State Board of Horticulture. Des Moines, IA: Mills & Co., 1871.

Page, Dave, and John Koblas. *F. Scott Fitzgerald in Minnesota: Toward the Summit*. St. Cloud, MN: North Star Press of St. Cloud, Inc., 1996.

Partsch, Tammy. *Nebraska City: Images of America*. Charleston, SC: Arcadia Publishing, 2015.

Portrait and Biographical Record of Shelby and Moultrie Counties, Illinois. Chicago: Biographical Publishing Co., 1891.

Rasdal, Dave. *Czech Village & New Bohemia: History in the Heartland*. Charleston, SC: The History Press, 2016.

Reser, William M. *Grist Mills of Tippecanoe County, Indiana*. N.p., 1945.

Rogers, Henry Wade, comp. *The Sidney Centennial Jubilee at Sidney Plains, Delaware Co., N.Y., June 13, 1872*. Ann Arbor, MI: Dr. Chase's Steam Printing House, 1875.

Smith, L. Bertrand. *Jesse Smith, His Ancestors and Descendants*. New York: Frank Allaben Genealogical Company, 1909.

Taylor, Charles Henry, ed. *History of the Board of Trade of the City of Chicago*. Vol. 3, part 1. Chicago: Robert O. Law Company, 1917.

Turner, Dorcas Johnston. *In Memoriam: Mary Jane Aldrich*. N.p., n.d.

United States Federal Trade Commission. *Report of the Federal Trade Commission on the Meat-Packing Industry*. Part III: "Methods of the Five Packers in Controlling the Meat-Packing Industry." Washington, D.C.: Government Printing Office, June 28, 1919.

"View of the Pork Packing Establishment of J.Y. Griffin & Co., Limited. Louise Bridge, Winnipeg, Man. (1904)." Image courtesy of University of Manitoba Archives and Special Collections. Available online at www.flickr.com/photos/manitobamaps/3131438168/in/photostream.

Walker, Charles I. *Pioneer Collections: Report of the Pioneer Society of the State of Michigan*. Vol. 4. Lansing, MI: W.S. George & Co. Printers and Binders, 1883.

Warren, Wilson J. *Tied to the Great Packing Machine: The Midwest and Meatpacking.* Iowa City: University of Iowa Press, 2007.

Watkins, Albert. *History of Nebraska: From the Earliest Explorations to the Present Time with Portraits, Maps, and Tables.* Vol. 3, first ed. Lincoln, NE: Western Publishing and Engraving Company, 1913.

Willard, Frances E., and Mary A. Livermore, eds. *A Woman of the Century: Fourteen Hundred-Seventy Biographical Sketches Accompanied by Portraits of Leading American Women in All Walks of Life.* Buffalo, NY: Charles Wells Moulton, 1893.

Woodhead, Lindy. *Shopping, Seduction & Mr. Selfridge.* New York: Random House Publishing Group, 2012.

Periodicals

Alliance Herald (NE), 1915.

The Annals of Iowa, 1911.

Beatrice Daily Sun (NE), 1928.

Bloomington Weekly Pantagraph (IL), 1893.

Cedar Rapids Evening Gazette, 1898.

Chicago Tribune, 1893, 1895, 1899, 1921.

Commercial and Financial Chronicle, 1906.

Courier-Journal (Louisville, KY), 1890.

Daily American (Nashville, TN), 1885.

Daily Inter Ocean (Chicago), 1894, 1895.

Durkee Family Newsletter, 1985.

Fort Wayne Daily Gazette, 1894, 1897.

Fort Wayne Sunday Gazette, 1897.

Fremont Tri-Weekly Tribune, 1899.

Gazette (Cedar Rapids, IA), 1899.

The Grand Rapids Furniture Record, 1922.

Journal of the Illinois State Historical Society, 1917.

Kansas City Star, 1937.

Lincoln Daily Star, 1917.

Lincoln Journal-Star, 1887, 1919, 1925, 2019.

Logansport Daily Reporter, 1892.

Logansport Pharos-Tribune, 1893.

Memphis Commercial, 1893.

Monmouth Daily Atlas (IL), 1922.

National Provisioner, 1907, 1908, 1910, 1911, 1912, 1914, 1916, 1917, 1919, 1922, 1924, 1925, 1926, 1928, 1929, 1930, 1935, 1936.

Nebraska Advertiser (Brownville, NE), 1871.

Nebraska City News, 1875, 1882, 1884, 1901, 1907, 1909, 1913, 1915, 1917, 1918, 1923.

Nebraska City News-Press, 1953, 1964.

Nebraska City Weekly News, 1924.

Nebraska Daily News-Press (Nebraska City, NE), 1926, 1927, 1928, 1929, 1930, 1931, 1932, 1933, 1934, 1936.

Nebraska Horticulture, 1921.

Nebraska Press (Lincoln, NE), year unknown.

Nebraska State Journal (Lincoln, NE), 1872, 1909, 1910.

Omaha Daily Bee, 1885, 1890.

Pittsburgh Post, 1897.

Reading Times (PA), 1909.

Record-Union (Sacramento, CA), 1886.

The Recruit: A Naval Pictorial Magazine, 1918.

Review (Decatur, IL), 1885.

St. Joseph Herald, 1893, 1895.

St. Joseph News-Press, 1907.

St. Louis Daily Globe, 1893.

St. Louis Magazine, 2014.

St. Louis Post-Dispatch, 1895.

St. Paul Globe, 1904.

Successful American, 1902.

Superior Express, 1927.

Syracuse Journal Democrat, 1934.

Victoria Daily Times (British Columbia), 1906.

Washington Times, 1894.

Winnipeg Tribune, 1905, 1906.

Online Sources

Coe College History: The First Hundred Years. public.coe.edu/historyweb/index.html.

Cottey College. cottey.edu.

Travelers Protective Association. www.tpahq.org.

Other

Cedar Rapids City Directory, 1869.
United States Censuses, 1870, 1910, 1920.

ABOUT THE AUTHOR

Rachel Brupbacher is a great-great-granddaughter of Carl Milton Aldrich and, through him, a descendant of some of Nebraska's earliest settlers. The fifth generation of her family to have lived in the "Tree Planter State," she graduated summa cum laude from a private Nebraska college with a bachelor of arts degree in French, German and history. In both this book and her first, *Miles Minor Kellogg and the Encinitas Boathouses* (The History Press, 2021), Rachel blends her love of storytelling with her passion for reviving the past.

Visit us at
www.historypress.com